# VIRGINIA

PORTRAITS OF AMERICA

# VIRGINIA

JOHN BOWEN

CHARTWELL
BOOKS, INC.

A QUINTET BOOK

Published by Chartwell Books Inc.,
A Division of Book Sales Inc.,
110 Enterprise Avenue,
Secaucus, New Jersey 07094

ISBN 0-89009-884-0

This book was designed and produced by
Quintet Publishing Limited
6 Blundell Street, London N7
in association with Footnote
Productions Limited

Art Director Peter Bridgewater
Editor Sheila Rosenzweig
Photographer Ian Howes

Typeset in Great Britain by
Leaper & Gard Limited, Bristol
Colour origination in Hong Kong by
Hong Kong Graphic Arts Company Limited,
Hong Kong
Printed in Hong Kong by Leefung-Asco
Printers Limited

For my father, whose roots
reach deep into Virginia's soil.

# CONTENTS

# VIRGINIA TRINITIES

*A* good photograph, like a painting, has certain characteristics: composition, depth, unity, and meaning. It requires personal interpretation. It is designed to please, but at the same time it must provide insight into the nature of the subject. Virginia presents a portrait of flawed beauty, created by topography, historical imperatives, people with visions and dreams, and even, at an odd moment, chance. There is, at the same time, a universal quality about the Virginia experience and a very particular pattern that makes the state unique.

To understand Virginia, one must inspect all its aspects, just as one does a good portrait. Virginia is the product of its three principal regions—the Tidewater, the Piedmont, and the mountains and valleys in the west—and of three tumultuous periods in history. It has had three political systems: it was a business, a colony, and a state. Virginia also has had a trinity of heroes—George Washington, Robert E. Lee, and Thomas J. "Stonewall" Jackson— and others who rate at least a glimpse of Mount Olympus. The final trinity is the religious one, which has exerted a strong influence. Understanding Virginia requires a knowledge of all these characteristics and a willingness to acknowledge that they all meet at some point in time or space.

The Tidewater region, on the coast, is, naturally, the oldest. The lowlands provide good farmland and good harbors. The region looks seaward, and always has. The only difference between the eras is how far to sea the people looked. Watermen populate the numerous coves of Chesapeake Bay and the towns along the major rivers—rivers whose depth and breadth startled settlers accustomed to the thin rivers of the Old World. As it always has, the land quickly produces wealth—for some—and promises to do the same for others. Economic opportunity created and sustained Virginia to such an extent that controls were among the first laws passed. The Indians did not always cooperate, and in 1622 launched a massive attempt to wipe out the colony.

Representative government sprouted and successfully resisted the efforts of a distant king to pull it up by its roots. The College of William and Mary attracted students like Thomas Jefferson, and easily became the intellectual arbiter of the state. Less than a century was required following the 1607 initial landing to produce a modest level of comfort in living. This gave men like George Mason, author of the Virginia Bill of Rights, which became a model for the national counterpart, and James Madison, whose thoughts framed the Constitution, time to ruminate on life and to formulate their ideas for a better society. When Virginians resisted British efforts to deprive them of democracy, they considered themselves better Englishmen than their mentors in the old country. Freedom and loyalty mingled freely for a time, then divided the state disastrously. When the Revolutionary War came, some of the rich planters along the James deserted their plantations, never to return. One who stayed, upon hearing of the British defeat at Trenton, in New Jersey, hanged himself. Two of America's first presidents were born in the same area.

The Piedmont gave the new colony room to expand. There, gentlemen farmers prospered on tobacco and neighborly conversation and tried to live in harmony with nature and man. Piedmonters sent individualists, including the fiery-tongued Patrick Henry, to the colonial legislature to contest for power with the Tidewater barons. Homes in the Piedmont were serviceable, but hardly mansions; the people worked hard and sometimes suffered greatly.

The mountains and valleys of the western part of the state are distinct geographical features, quite different from the lowlands of the coast and the Piedmont. West of the Shenandoah Valley, the mountains stretch the length of the state from north to south, and for a time retarded the movement of people westward. East of the valley, the mountains graduate southward into foothills that permitted the creation of towns at Roanoke and Bristol. The people who inhabited the mountains and valleys were distinct, too. Although some had followed the rivers and trails westward from the coast, others filtered down the Shenandoah Valley from Pennsylvania. The Germans, with their Lutheranism, and the Scotch-Irish with their Presbyterianism, worshipped differently from the Anglicans in Tidewater, and even from most of the nonconformists in the Piedmont. Life in the west was not easy, and at times the Indians were especially cruel and violent. The political dominance of the eastern part of the state was resented, but the fires of

NOVA BRITANNIA,
## OFFERING MOST
Excellent fruites by Planting in
VIRGINIA.

Exciting all such as be well affected
to further the same.

LONDON
Printed for SAMVEL MACHAM, and are to be sold at
his Shop in Pauls Church-yard, at the
Signe of the Bul-head.
1609.

The **title-page** of a promotion tract published in London in 1609 tempts fortune-seeking Englishmen across the seas to the plantations of the first New World English colony in Virginia.

**Opposite** Sunset is a special time as an explosion of quiet colors envelops the Chincoteague harbor on the Eastern Shore.

8

A fishing boat, crab pots and nets on a dock **center** demonstrate the importance of seafood to the life of Chincoteague Islanders on the isolated Eastern Shore.

independence burned hotter in frontiersmen than in the intellectuals in Williamsburg. They were not thinkers, they were men of action, and their physical commitment to freedom would soon set an example for those who debated freedom in Raleigh Tavern or Chowning's in Williamsburg.

As Professor Marshall Fishwick of Washington and Lee University pointed out, the early history of Virginia is characterized by an east-west pull, not the north-south division that influenced the nation. That east-west pull might have been greater, and Virginia might have had more than three principal regions, had not history intervened. The original charter gave the Virginia Company dominion over the land that extended from sea to sea and from the Cape Fear River in North Carolina to Maine. Virginia never laid claim to most of this land, voluntarily surrendered the Northwest Territory, which extended as far as Michigan, and then lost West Virginia during the Civil War. This left the triangle shape that exists today.

Williamsburg **right** was the capital of Virginia from 1699 to 1779. The Williamsburg Historic District contains nearly 500 eighteenth-century buildings that have been either restored or reconstructed to their original appearance. Costumed attendants are available to answer questions and crafts of the period are demonstrated in dozens of workshops.

## Subregions of the State

And although the basic three-part division created by nature remains, several subregions developed. The Eastern Shore, Virginia's share of the peninsula that also includes part of Maryland and the state of Delaware, is a distinct section of the Tidewater region. Rivers flowing into the Chesapeake Bay divide the mainland of Tidewater into enclaves—the south shore of Hampton Roads (Norfolk, Virginia Beach, Chesapeake, and Portsmouth and their hinterland); the Virginia Peninsula (Newport News, Hampton, the historic triangle of Jamestown, Williamsburg, and Yorktown, and several counties); the Middle Peninsula, principally Gloucester and Middlesex counties and the town of West Point; the Northern Neck, the birthplace of Washington and the

The 18-room Georgian mansion at Mount Vernon **left** was George Washington's beloved home from 1754 until his death in 1799. Visitors to the preserved plantation, formal gardens and Washington family tomb have been welcome since 1858.

The meanderings of mountain-top Skyline Drive produce many magnificent panoramas such as this one **center**. Overlooks along the 105-mile route make sightseeing safe and easy.

The **bald eagle**, with its distinctive white head and tail feathers, has a massive yellow beak and a wingspread up to eight feet. It is the national bird of the United States.

Lees; Richmond, the state's capital and alter ego; and Northern Virginia, the suburbs of Washington, D.C., easily the most liberal area of the state.

The Piedmont breaks roughly into two sub-regions. Southside and the central Piedmont. The western area cannot be divided into contiguous areas, but can be separated by geographical feature into mountains, the long, lean Shenandoah Valley, and the southwest, containing the state's highest peak, Mount Rogers, and the city of Bristol, which straddles the Tennessee border.

The influence of the geographical trinity is at least equaled by the effects of the three major historical periods: the colonial and revolutionary period, the Civil War and Reconstruction, and the period since World War II. Each in its own way helped determine Virginia's attitude toward the nation and the concepts that have divided Americans. The first two made Virginia insular and unique, the third made it less so.

Virginia shares an English heritage with other eastern states, so what makes it different? It was the first colony, and thus the founder of the nation—a corporate form of primogeniture, so to speak. It took only a quarter-century to create the form of society—economic, political, religious, and social—that would dominate the first important period in the state's history. The concept of representative government took root at Jamestown, and Virginians would never give it up. The House of Burgesses met first in 1619, only little more than a decade after the founding of the colony, but representative government was already entrenched by that time. Virginians were quick to revolt—Bacon's Rebellion preceded the Revolutionary War by almost a century—but were so loyal to the British crown that Charles II bestowed upon the state its most cherished and longest-lasting nickname, the "Old Dominion". When the break with the crown finally came, no state contributed more to the struggle or suffered more than Virginia. Virginia's leadership was important; historians generally agree that the reputation of George Washington and his perseverance as a commander held together an army of citizen-soldiers who would much rather have been tending their fields or blacksmithing. Washington made the political commitment a military reality at Yorktown,

where Lord Cornwallis surrendered his British and Hessian army. Without that victory, the Declaration of Independence would have been but a footnote to history. Washington was destined to set an equally uplifting example in peace. Once again, he left the place he loved most, Mount Vernon, to answer the call to duty. He rode his horse to New York to become the nation's first president, stayed two terms, and resisted efforts to keep him there longer. In his final address, he established a principle of avoiding foreign entanglements that was to be national policy for more than a century and would become a permanent part of the national psyche.

The Civil War had no less an impact on Virginia. The state provided the Confederacy's most famous leader, General Robert E. Lee, and loaned its capital as the capital of the Confederacy. The first battles were fought on Virginia soil, and the roll call of battlefields eventually included hitherto isolated places such as Manassas (also known as Bull Run), Cold Harbor, Wilderness, and New Market, and well-known places like Petersburg, Richmond, and Fredericksburg. When Lee surrendered to General Ulysses S. Grant at Appomattox, hardened soldiers wept and went home to face the rigors of occupation. The Civil War and Reconstruction structured Virginia's life for at least seventy years after the fighting stopped.

It is difficult to say when modern Virginia was born. It may have been when John D. Rockefeller, Jr., decided to restore Colonial Williamsburg, an act that reminded Virginians of the rich heritage before the Civil War and offered a glimpse of the promises of the modern era, or it may have been when Virginians suffered the hardships of the depression era. Revival had begun by the time World War II broke out, and it accelerated after the war. In-migration increased the state's population by 73 percent in the postwar period, enlarging an already substantial non-native segment. By 1970, two-thirds of the population was urban, a reversal of the traditional situation. The 1980 census counted a population of 5.6 million, but showed also that Virginia is only partly industrialized. Although the largest single employer in the state is the Newport News Shipbuilding and Drydock Company, with twenty-nine thousand employees, agriculture remains the state's dominant industry, with

**Robert E. Lee**, shown here in a pre-war photograph, was appointed commander-in-chief of Virginia's naval and military forces on 23 April, 1861, and raised to the rank of major-general.

tourism in second place. A rising standard of living sent Virginians outside the state to study and to experience the various ways of the world.

In-migration, urbanization, and a revolution in communications weakened, but did not destroy, Virginia's historical allegiance to the Southern viewpoint. Urban Virginians generally consider themselves part of a border state, while the more conservative rural areas cling to old traditions. When author Parke Rouse, Jr., of Williamsburg titled one of his books *Below the James Lies Dixie*, he recognized the changed personality of the state. Nearly all the major Civil War battles in Virginia were fought north of that line.

Although the Virginia portrait signifies change, that does not mean that Virginia's devotion to history is dead. It is impossible to understand Virginia without recognizing the continuing impact of history upon it. History markers are everywhere. Citizens in almost every community are organized in some manner to hold onto the past, and their tenaciousness could set an example for any environmentalist group. History is discussed in reverent terms, and few politicians are willing to risk the wrath of the local historical society in Richmond, Hampton, or elsewhere. The Virginia Society for the Preservation of Antiquities, Daughters of the Confederacy, Colonial Dames, Daughters of the American Revolution, and many more groups have exerted a positive influence to protect remnants of history from a throwaway society. They are responsible for the existence of many old structures, including Mount Vernon. Williamsburg's Scottish descendants support two ancestral organizations, the Saint Andrews Society and the Balmoral Society.

*Famous Virginians*

It may also be impossible to understand Virginia without some feeling for family connections. The Lees and Byrds have given prominent leadership to the state for more than two hundred years. Robert E. Lee had distinguished predecessors—Richard Henry, "Light-Horse Harry", and Francis Lightfoot Lee, all Revolutionary War heroes. The Byrds along the James River were synonymous with colonial life, and Senators Harry Flood Byrd, Sr., and Harry Flood Byrd, Jr., represented Virginia in the United States Senate for more than forty years in this century. They were titular heads of what was known as the "Byrd Machine."

Virginians have been prominent in politics and the military from the beginning of the country's history. In the darkest hour of the first year of the colony, the citizens abandoned their noble governor for the discipline represented by Captain John Smith. He pulled them through, but never became popular. Virginians founded the first representative government in America during the seventeen years the colony was a commercial enterprise. Fourteen men held the reins of power during that period, most with the consent of the governed. The royal era that followed, broken by six years as a commonwealth during the Cromwell period in England, could not change that. The state still describes itself as a commonwealth. Virginia politicians helped foment the Revolutionary War; names like Washington, Thomas Jefferson, Patrick Henry, James Madison, and George Wythe are household words. Virginia has been called the "Mother of Presidents" as Virginians Washington, Jefferson, Madison, James Monroe, William Henry Harrison, John Tyler, Zachary Taylor, and Woodrow Wilson were elected to office. Wilson, the only Virginian since the Civil War to become president, was governor of New Jersey before being elected president.

Wartime heroes are a specialty for Virginia. In addition to Washington, the Lees, and Jacksons, men like George Rogers Clark, Winfield Scott, J.E.B. Stuart, and Joseph E. Johnston left lasting legacies. General George C. Marshall, World War II chief of staff and postwar diplomat, graduated from Virginia Military Institute. General Douglas MacArthur was supposed to have been a Virginian, but arrived prematurely as his mother prepared to return to her native Norfolk for his birth. He chose Virginia as his final resting place.

Ever since the restless John Smith explored the Indian lands around Jamestown, Virginians have been a curious people. Meriwether Lewis and William Clark connected the two

A London firm advertises its Indian connections
on this **Virginia tobacco label**. Tobacco became so
important a staple of the Virginian economy
that for a while it was used as a basis for currency.

coasts of the United States by a cross-continent trek in the early nineteenth century. In the latter half of that century, Commodore Matthew Fontaine Maury earned the title "Pathfinder of the Seas." Not far behind was Admiral Richard Evelyn Byrd, the first man to fly over the North and South Poles. Dr. Walter Reed went from rural Gloucester County to Cuba to conquer yellow fever.

Virginia history can be interpreted through her authors. The state has a literary tradition that started with its well-educated settlers. One gets the impression that every colonist wanted to write—about himself. Captain John Smith left a book that, four hundred years later, still causes historians to break out in cold argument. William Byrd and Governor Alexander Spotswood were early writers. In the nineteenth century, the tragic but talented Edgar Allan Poe and the whimsical Thomas Nelson Page showed the contrast between the two halves of the century. Novelists Ellen Glasgow and Willa Cather foretold the reminiscing of James Branch Cabell and the scholarship of Douglas Southall Freeman. Two of the nation's most talented writers of today, Tom Wolfe and William Styron, are Virginians.

Although Virginians have tended toward the martial and fine arts, they have not neglected education and science. The nation's first free school was founded in Hampton in the seventeenth century. The state is dotted with colleges and universities that date back to the eighteenth and early nineteenth centuries. Booker T. Washington left a slave cabin in Franklin County to become a national inspiration as an educator. Cyrus Hall McCormick found time at a grist mill in Rockbridge County to invent the mechanical reaper, the machine that produced an agricul-

tural revolution on the great plains of the Midwest. Virginians were on hand at many historic moments in aviation, and when President Dwight David Eisenhower initiated the space program, a large role was assigned to the Langley Research Center at Hampton. The men who exhibited "The Right Stuff" took their baby steps in space from there. Hampton remembers the Mercury Seven by naming bridges after them.

Virginians do not offer their affection lightly. In the more than three hundred and seventy-five years the state has existed, only two men have been accorded honorary citizenship: the Marquis de Lafayette, a Revolutionary War hero, and John D. Rockefeller, Jr. The heroes that Virginia reveres are substantial men and women, not tinsel and promise. They are, above all, persons of character and good reputation, and if they come from a "good" family, so much the better. Many Virginians still feel good breeding is likely to tell. Virginians have not completely abandoned what Professor Fishwick calls the Chesapeake trinity—wealth, status, and privilege.

For all its self-adulation, Virginia generally has been an open society. The life-style does not exclude outsiders, it converts them. Virginia is usually regarded as a uniquely British creation, but that is only partly true. The British settlers learned from the Indians, who already had an organized society and an agrarian economy based on corn planted in the river bottoms. The settlement at Jamestown was not limited to Anglo-Saxons. Only a year after the English arrived, came Poles, to work in the glassworks. Black slaves soon followed, and Huguenots from France helped the colony expand. A few Irish and Welsh came, too, and many went inland. Germans and Scotch-Irish drifted down the Shenandoah Valley, and a few Hessians remained after the war to help populate the frontier. Peter Francisco, a Virginian of Portuguese descent, was one of the state's most popular Revolutionary War heroes.

If Virginians tend to think of their state as heaven on earth, they may be forgiven. Historical precedence was established by none other than the well-travelled Captain John Smith, who wrote: "Heaven and Earth never agreed better to frame a place for man's habitation."

# TIDEWATER TIES

**Tobacco** was first cultivated as a crop in Virginia in 1612 and by 1620 it had become one of the colony's leading exports. The original plant was a fast-burning, mild-flavored variety called *Nicotiana rustica*.

he dictionary defines Tidewater as the coastal area whose streams are affected by the rise and fall of ocean and bay tides and whose water, consequently, is brackish. Virginians accept the dictionary definition as one of their lesser alternatives. For them, Tidewater is always spelled with a capital T, and the word can be applied to areas of varying dimensions. The historical Tidewater Virginia extends beyond the limit of tidal action, generally to the fall line of the rivers. Since the fall line formed a natural barrier to early colonization, the population built up rapidly below it. The economy of early Virginia was based on tobacco, and beyond the fall line it was difficult to send to market the pungent leaves literally worth their weight in gold. Thus, the great plantations grew along the riverbanks near the coast and developed into a close-knit society based on trade and a European orientation. The area is loaded with place names taken directly from the mother country of England—Surry, York, Isle of Wight, Hampton—or names honoring royalty of the colonial period.

Though linguistically incorrect, the historical tidewater has definite boundaries. That is not true of two other uses of the word Tidewater. The first defines a triangle a hundred miles wide at the base along the North Carolina boundary and narrow at the apex near Washington, D.C., which is somewhat smaller than the historical Tidewater. The other, whose use is limited to the Norfolk area, describes the south side of Hampton Roads, principally the cities of Norfolk, Virginia Beach, Portsmouth, and Chesapeake. Tidewater residents somehow are able to keep all this straight, but it can be confusing to outsiders. Thus, in this book, all references will be to the historical Tidewater, which is the one most easily understood even in Virginia.

Tidewater has a distinct life-style, dictated in part by nature and in part by its precedence as the first area to be settled. The area is naturally water-oriented, as it has been throughout its existence. Sheltered harbors, deep water, and a necessity to trade have created substantial port cities. In addition, every cove has docks where commercial and

Achilles harbor **right** is typical of the numerous coves in Gloucester County which provide safe anchorage for the small fishermen. These picturesque and profitable places are being crowded by residential development.

**Opposite** Cape Charles, one of the principal towns on the Eastern Shore, takes on an idyllic appearance at dusk. It is both a seafood port and market for the nearby farms.

Going out is an adventure everytime. The hard life of a crab fisherman requires a special breed of man **above**. Jurisdictional disputes among the states bordering on Chesapeake Bay have persisted since the founding of the nation.

The crab boats on Monday Creek ride easily after a hard day's work **right**. Finfishing and shellfishing have been important to the Tidewater region throughout its history.

The **Canada goose**, the most widespread goose in North America, is readily identified by its white 'chin strap' and the sharp contrast between its black neck and pale breast.

pleasure boats mingle, and a coterie of plain-speaking watermen who love the sea so much they spend most of their time ashore admiring it. Good seafood is more than a tradition: it is a must. Many of the old houses have widow's walks, and every man who owns a boat is called "Captain." The docks smell of seafood, and the communities that back up this water style have a parochial attitude.

Tidewater shares with Maryland both the two-hundred-mile-long Chesapeake Bay and the Potomac River, and it has been an uneasy partnership. Watermen of the two states have contested rights to the river and bay from the earliest days—and not always peacefully. One of the early U.S. Supreme Court decisions concerned those rights. The days of gunfire in the night have ended, but oystermen still argue about whether hand or patent tongs are permissible, whether dredges should be used to harvest clams, and who has the right to put crab pots where. The seafood industry is important in the commercial life of Tidewater Virginia.

The historical Tidewater was shaped to an extraordinary degree by topography. The landmass is divided by Chesapeake Bay and four great rivers (the James, York, Rappahannock, and Potomac) into a series of peninsulas and enclaves. The enclaves lie at both ends, at North Carolina and Washington. Between the James and York rivers is the Virginia Peninsula, an imprecise but simple name that results from precedence and not from snobbery. The Middle Peninsula lies between the York and Rappahannock rivers, and the Northern Neck stands between the Rappahannock and Potomac rivers. Hampton Roads, the body of water between the entrance to Chesapeake Bay and the mouth of the James River, is one of the world's greatest natural harbors.

Since intercourse across the wide waters was difficult, each peninsula developed in its own way. Life in eastern Virginia was oriented in an east-west direction well into the twentieth century, as migration and commerce followed the lines of least resistance, first to the Piedmont and then to the mountains. Although passenger boats established regular routes on the Chesapeake Bay, these could not compete with the easier land routes. Even with a ferry crossing the five-mile-wide **river** between Newport News and Norfolk, to those on the mainland Richmond seemed closer

The 17.6-mile Chesapeake Bay Bridge–Tunnel **left**, which crosses the mouth of Chesapeake Bay, is one of the man-made wonders of the world. It provides the primary physical connection between mainland Virginia and the Eastern Shore.

though it was eighty miles away. The isolation of the peninsulas began to disappear in the 1920s, when a bridge was built across the James from Newport News to Surry County. It was not a profitable idea, but it was prophetic. The 1950s would see bridges tie together all the peninsulas. A few years later, tunnels connected the Virginia Peninsula and the Norfolk area and the south side of Hampton Roads to the Eastern Shore.

## Tidewater Towns

This geographic division also determined economic growth patterns. Norfolk was a major colonial port, along with City Point (now Hopewell) on the James River, Yorktown on the York River, Urbanna and Fredericksburg on the Rappahannock River, and Alexandria on the Potomac. The pattern has not changed much. Newport News and Richmond have developed, and Fredericksburg and Urbanna no longer are ports for oceangoing vessels. Although American industry began with the glassworks at Jamestown and the iron furnace at Falling Creek, the Tidewater did not attract industry for long. Tobacco became such an important crop that laws had to be passed to keep craftsmen from abandoning their trades to seek their fortunes on farms. Land was cheap, and that set the agricultural pattern that predominates even today. Thus, the region was late to industrialize, and most of the industry came with the railroads. The city of Newport News, for example, was founded in the late nineteenth century as the terminus of the Chesapeake and Ohio Railroad and as home of a new shipyard. A heavy concentration of military bases formed around Hampton Roads, the result of a good harbor and historical decisions, particularly during the series of wars that started with the Civil War. More than a dozen bases housing all the services are located around Hampton Roads, including the Atlantic headquarters of the North Atlantic Treaty Organization (SACLANT), the Armed Forces Staff College in Norfolk, and the Coast

Fishing boats ride easily
at docks in Chincoteague. Despite the
extensive coastline on the
Eastern Shore and the dedication of the
watermen, agriculture has
replaced fishing as the dominant industry.

More than 275 kinds of
birds have been spotted in the Chincoteague
National Wildlife Refuge.
Several kinds of herons, egrets, ducks, hawks,
rail, plovers, sandpipers,
and terns are among them.

The **black skimmer**, which inhabits coastal regions, uses the sharp elongated lower part of its beak to snatch prey from the water.

Guard Officers' Candidate School at York-town. In both world wars, millions of men marched to and from ships at the Hampton Roads port of embarkation. A permanent Victory Arch stands in Newport News over the route to the waiting ships.

Cities and towns dominate Tidewater today, a reversal of the traditional situation. A trend toward urbanization has eliminated several former counties. Norfolk is the state's largest city and its biggest port. In the more than three hundred and seventy-five years since Virginia was founded, the state capital has moved twice, without leaving Tidewater. It was relocated from Jamestown to Middle Plantation, now Williamsburg, for safety during wartime, and from Williamsburg to Richmond for the same season. Richmond never gave it up for long after that.

The divisions of Tidewater did not prevent the development of certain unifying characteristics. The region as a whole shares its unique history and has maintained extraordinary fondness for the mother country. Although the elite no longer send their sons to England for an education, as they did in the colonial days, Britain certainly stands at the top of every Virginia tourist's itinerary in Europe. Intellectual intercourse between the two countries has never ceased, and was enhanced by the celebrations connected with the bicentennial of American independence. Like it or not, Tidewater has embraced conformity, including the Anglican (Episcopalian) influence, more than have other regions of the state. Graciousness and hospitality still are important qualities.

## The Eastern Shore

The Eastern Shore deserves special mention since it was even more isolated than other Tidewater regions. It occupies seventy miles of the Delmarva peninsula, which it shares with part of Maryland and the state of Delaware. For most of its existence, until the 1960s, the Eastern Shore had no fixed connec-

A deer, protected on Assateague Island **center**, comes out at dusk. Animals roam the island, but visitors are confined to specified areas.

Carving duck decoys **left** has been raised to the status of a folk art in recent years, as more and more are made for display rather than the traditional use as a lure for flying ducks. Dozens of Eastern Shore carvers create a wide variety of attractive painted wood decoys.

tion to the mainland of Virginia, and thus was socially and economically oriented more toward Maryland than to Virginia. The people of the Eastern Shore nevertheless cherished their Virginia citizenship and defended it fiercely. The completion of the 17.6-mile Chesapeake Bay Bridge-Tunnel in 1964 gave the Eastern Shore the fixed connection to the mainland that it had long sought, and brought new traffic to the "Ocean Hiway" (Routes 13–17), which passes through the area on its way from Maine to Florida. It is incidental to those on the Eastern Shore that the bridge-tunnel across the mouth of Chesapeake Bay is regarded as one of the engineering wonders of the modern world.

The Eastern Shore is predominately agricultural, and is especially known for vegetables and poultry. The seafood industry makes the docks of Cape Charles, Onancock, and Chincoteague the most important features of those communities. Chincoteague has an annual Oyster Festival, but is best known for the pony penning each July, in which the wild ponies from Assateague Island are rounded up. The area does not object to

Little-known Wallops Island Station of the National Aeronautics and Space Administration **overleaf** has played an important role in scientific experiments in space. A museum depicting the history of manned flight is open to the public.

Assateague's wild ponies **above**, **below** and **opposite below**, stunted descendants of horses shipwrecked in the seventeenth century, roam free on the marshy island most of the year. An annual roundup benefits the Chincoteague Volunteer Fire Department and provides an opportunity for the well-known Chincoteague Pony Penning festival.

The **osprey**, found throughout the country near lakes, rivers and coastal waters, hovers with beating wings before diving feet-first into water to catch its prey.

the settlement their of retirees interested in pleasure-boating, but it is less comfortable with a new industry, the search for oil off the Virginia coast.

The Eastern Shore was among the first places in Tidewater to be settled, and thus has numerous historic relics. Records in the Northampton County Courthouse, restored to its 1731 appearance, go back to 1632. Hungars Parish, the first on the Shore, is not far away. The present church building dates from 1750. Frances Makemie, who brought Presbyterianism to Tidewater, is buried on the Eastern Shore.

Around Accomac, the seat of the county spelled somewhat differently, Accomack, are several examples of restored colonial houses. Seven Gables was built in 1786; Warwick, partly burned during the Revolutionary War, has been restored to approximate the 1700 original.

Despite misgivings about the new oil invasion, the Shore has welcomed another modern institution. The Wallops Island station of the National Aeronautics and Space Administration is both an active launch facility and a tourist attraction. The visitors' center houses

a small collection of spacecraft and aircraft items and visual graphics dealing with the progress in space.

The Eastern Shore is outdoors country, where large areas remained virtually unused right into the modern era. This has made the use of many areas, such as the Barrier Islands, a source of controversy between environmentalists and developers. Many of the wetlands areas are protected by law, and the Chincoteague National Wildlife Refuge and Assateague Island National Seashore preserve important outdoor areas.

## Norfolk

Norfolk, the state's largest city, is the self-proclaimed leader of Tidewater. Although this claim may be resented by others, both history and financial clout support the claim. Norfolk

Shellfishing is a way of life on Virginia's Eastern Shore **left** and boats developed especially to hunt oysters, clams and crabs have existed since the earliest days of the nation. Oyster shells paved roads before asphalt became standard.

**Whittle House, Norfolk**, bears the confident, neo-classical influences which characterized the domestic architecture of Norfolk when the town was rebuilt after a devastating fire in 1776.

also has made a conscious effort to shed its "navy town" image without offending either the navy or the sailors, and has had some success in doing so. Gone are downtown streets that once were infamous, and in their place stand tall, modern bank headquarters and hotels. Family-style entertainment has replaced the gaudy burlesque houses, nearby residential areas such as Ghent have been upgraded, and a new waterside development has revived interest in activities along the Elizabeth River. This redevelopment was not out of character. The appearance of Norfolk has changed several times during its history, and not always by choice. It was burned during the Revolutionary War and had to be rebuilt almost from scratch. The historic gem that survived the burning, 1739 St. Paul's Episcopal Church, also was saved during the redevelopment and remains the cornerstone of historic preservation in the downtown area. The church is a fine example of colonial architecture, but is best known for the Revolutionary War cannonball imbedded in the southeast wall. The 1792 Moses Myers House depicts the life-style of a successful shipowner in the eighteenth century; the Willoughby-Baylor

**Overleaf** Assateague Island hosts two national parks—the Chincoteague National Wildlife Refuge in Virginia and the Assateague National Seashore in Maryland. The lighthouse, when built in 1863, was the second strongest on the East Coast.

27

St. Paul's Episcopal Church **right** survived the burning of Norfolk in the late eighteenth century, but absorbed a permanent cannonball in the War of 1812.

Freemason Street **below** and **opposite below** was one of Norfolk's earliest residential streets, but now is part of the redeveloped downtown section.

House was owned by a middle-class merchant of the same period.

General of the Armies Douglas MacArthur, a hero in two world wars and the Korean conflict, would have been an appropriate Tidewater hero. He combined both the irascible temperament of Captain John Smith and the sublime confidence of Robert E. Lee. He would have been born in Norfolk had he not been a premature baby. He arrived in Little Rock, Arkansas, while his mother was preparing to return to her Norfolk home for his birth. MacArthur chose Norfolk as his final resting place. He is entombed under the classical dome of the MacArthur Memorial, surrounded by his battle flags and some of his more memorable statements, including the "I shall return" promise made to the Philippines during World War II. The memorial also houses hundreds of mementoes, among them his medals, famous corncob pipe and slouched hat, papers, documents, photographs, paintings, and valuable gifts from world leaders, including the Emperor of Japan.

Norfolk also has made a major cultural commitment. Chrysler Museum, built around the private collection of industrialist Walter

For two centuries the Norfolk waterfront **above** and **middle** has been the principal port of Virginia. The area has taken on a new vitality. Skyscrapers tower above the water's edge. The Norfolk Naval Base, the largest in the world, is home port to more than a hundred ships of the U.S. Navy, including submarines and nuclear-powered aircraft carriers.

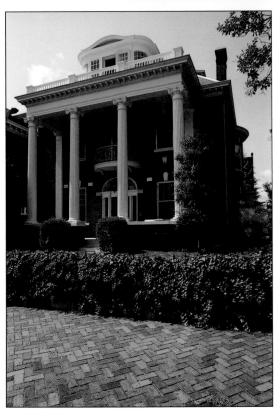

Chrysler and augmented by other sizable donations, ranks among the top twenty art museums in the nation. The older Hermitage Museum specializes in Oriental art, and has a superior collection of Chinese jade. A renaissance in restaurants and dinner theater has helped improve the Norfolk image, and Scope Convention and Cultural Center is a popular attraction. Annual festivals include rapidly growing Harborfest and the prestigious Azalea festival, which picks its queen from a different NATO country each year. The site of the festival is the city's Azalea Gardens, whose official name of Norfolk Botanical Gardens is usually ignored by resident and visitor alike. The Cousteau Society has chosen Norfolk as home base.

Ocean View is a distinct section of Norfolk because it once was a separate community. The resort has a long beach that attracts residents and visitors less affluent than those who go to Virginia Beach, and it also has excellent facilities for deep-sea fishing and pleasure-boating. Ocean View is the southern terminus of the Hampton Roads Bridge-Tunnel, which connects the Norfolk area to the Virginia Peninsula. The tunnel passes under a channel

31

Dr. William Selden built
Selden's Point as a summer home in 1807 in
Norfolk. The house was
used as Union army headquarters during the
occupation of Norfolk during
the Civil War, while Dr. Selden was serving as
surgeon general of the
Confederacy.

The General Douglas MacArthur
Memorial is a museum and research center.
MacArthur's crypt is surrounded
by battle flags and some of his famous
sayings, including his "I
shall return" promise to the Philippines.

The Willoughby-Baylor House **below**, a mixture of Federal and Georgian architecture, captures the lifestyle of a middle-class merchant in the late eighteenth century. It has been refurnished according to an inventory made in 1800.

This elegant riverside mansion **right** houses the Hermitage Foundation Museum in Norfolk. Its Oriental collection is outstanding.

for oceangoing ships bound for the ports of Norfolk, Portsmouth, Newport News, and Richmond. Upstream from the bridge-tunnel, merchant ships from around the world and navy vessels anchor; normally a dozen or more may be visible from almost any vantage point and from the tour boats that cruise the harbor.

## Virginia Beach

Virginia Beach is one of the principal waterfront resorts on the East Coast. Although merger with adjacent Princess Anne County into the present city of Virginia Beach changed its character somewhat, the city still depends largely on the tourist trade. Back from the beach diversions range from a skateboard bowl in one of the city's parks to the seventeenth-century Adam Thoroughgood House, which may be the oldest surviving home in the

Norfolk's Chrysler Museum **left**, founded in 1933, is regarded as one of the twenty best in the United States. Its permanent collection includes all major American and European art periods, as well as ancient artifacts and decorative arts.

Virginia Beach **below** is a haven for lovers of water sports. The miles of delightful shoreline are perfect for launching sailboats and windsurfers.

**Overleaf** A three-mile-long boardwalk parallels the wide, sandy beach at Virginia Beach. The famous Norwegian Lady figurehead commemorates the wreck in 1891 of the Norwegian bark *Dictator*. A similar statue stands in Foss, Norway.

35

A comely lifeguard **above** watches the swimming and surfing at Virginia Beach, one of the premier ocean resorts on the East Coast of the United States.

Virginia Beach is a fun place, as these festival participants **right** show. The city, founded as an Atlantic Ocean resort, now encompasses a large and diverse region.

United States. Restored to its seventeenth-century appearance, the house recalls the life-style of a self-made man in the new colony. It has "beasties" or animal figures believed to protect the home from ill fortune and a formal garden, a popular affectation of the nouveau riche even in the colonial period. Two highly prized relics are leather ale mugs, shaped like barmaids. They were given by Princess Anne to innkeeper John Ashford in 1729.

Thoroughgood, one of the colony's earliest entrepreneurs, also believed in a custom Virginians adopted from the mother country—marrying well. He came to Virginia as an indentured servant, completed his time, and returned to England to marry the daughter of a rich merchant. Whether the merchant was influenced by a scheme Thoroughgood devised to amass land is not known, but Adam and wife became rich by importing indentured servants, each of which brought him a grant of fifty acres.

Virginia Beach has been recognized nationally for one conservation project. A mound created by a trash dump has been made into a recreational area, with a race-course for the Soapbox Derby, a lake for paddle-wheel boats, and other facilities. It is appropriately named Mount Trashmore. The Cape Henry section of the city is known for two things: the 2,670-acre Seashore State Park, where the visitor can really escape from the rush of urban living, and the Cape Henry Memorial, located on an active military base.

The memorial commemorates the first landing of English settlers in Virginia on April 26, 1607, before they moved on to create the permanent colony at Jamestown.

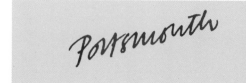

Portsmouth, one of Virginia's oldest communities, has an uneven history. In recent years, it has actively courted industrialization, embarked upon ambitious downtown redevelopment programs, and undergone a modest cultural renaissance. Naval history and Coastguard museums are located on the waterfront. One of Portsmouth's charms is its

role as the gateway to Dismal Swamp, whose nomenclature and appearance are both misleading. Dismal Swamp has coffee-colored water, often impenetrable tangles of trees and vines, and an assortment of snakes and animals. William Byrd II turned aside while serving as a commissioner to survey the Virginia-North Carolina boundary. But the swamp is far more hospitable than it seems. The water is dark from tannin from trees, but is said to be pure. It was used by early ships crews and settlers. George Washington surveyed the swamp without serious mishap, and each year thousands of hunters and tourists explore the shadows and natural quiet of this fascinating aberration of nature.

## The Smithfield Area

The hinterland south of the James is farm country, populated by whites and blacks who think conservatively and regard outsiders with some degree of suspicion. This is true even in the cities of Suffolk, Franklin, and Smithfield. Make-do has been a way of life since the Indians settled there ten thousand years ago, and it was a necessity during the colonial period. Peanuts are the principal crop, but roadside stands also sell melons, freshly picked vegetables, and fruit in season. Surry County is one of the few places where peanut and raisin pie can be found, but strong-tasting Smithfield ham has a national reputation. The packing houses are Smithfield's only big industry.

Smithfield, the largest community in Isle of Wight County, was settled during the first years of the Jamestown colony, but languished until it became a county seat in 1749. After that, it was a center of farm commerce and a port on the Pagan River. Isle of Wight's most famous historic structure, Saint Luke's Episcopal Church, often is associated with Smithfield because it is located near the town's limits. A survey of Virginia architecture conducted by the Virginia Museum in 1968 confirmed the uncertain date of the Saint

The Dismal Swamp **center**, now a popular tourist destination, has alternately attracted and repelled men throughout history. George Washington surveyed it, and ships obtained water there, but border surveyors in the 1700s turned aside.

This compact home in Virginia Beach, the Adam Thoroughgood House **below**, may be the oldest brick residence in the United State. It recreates the lifestyle of the early 1600s, when it was built, right down to the superstitious "beasties" supposed to ward off evil.

The **Virginia rail**, which inhabits fresh and brackish marshes, is no bigger than a meadowlark and is the only small rail to sport a long, slender bill.

A wealth of Victorian houses
attest to expansion in Smithfield during that
period. Some of the area's
wealth was associated with the flavorful Smithfield
ham.

The many fine homes in
Smithfield have been constructed over a long
period. It is not unusual
to see homes from different centuries
standing near each other.

Historic St. Luke's Episcopal Church **right** near Smithfield is the oldest original Gothic structure in America. Built in the mid-eighteenth century, it is preserved as an architectural monument but also continues as an active church.

Chippokes Plantation in Surry County **middle** has been farmed continuously since the seventeenth century. This manor house dates from the nineteenth century, but other buildings were constructed in the 1600s.

**Opposite** Surry Courthouse is a reconstruction, built in 1921-22, of the late nineteenth-century building that burned. It is the fifth courthouse on the site, and the seventh in the county's long history.

The **Virginia pine**, sometimes called the Scrub pine, has a long, narrow cone with prickly scales, recognizably different from the shorter and smoother cone of the Jack pine.

Luke's Church building. Three dates—1632, 1665 and 1682—are listed. No matter, Saint Luke's Church is the oldest original gothic structure in the nation and a splendid example of the cultural heritage imported from England by the first settlers. The red brick church, with stubby gothic tower, could have been transplanted from the English countryside. The interior is a mixture of innovative use of indigenous materials, such as the baptismal font hewn from a log, and import items, such as the silver bowl that held the water. The Pocahontas memorial window is half-hidden by stairs to a choir loft, and mention is made of a common colonial custom—secondary use of the building as a courthouse and meeting hall. Although still in use for worship, the church is maintained as a historic structure by the Saint Luke's Foundation.

The section of Tidewater that parallels the south shore of the James River may have more historical markers per mile than any other highway. Chippokes Plantation preserves one of the few original patents still intact and provides a glimpse of two key periods in the life of the area. The Clapboard House, which dates from 1644, is part of a living colonial farm maintained on the site. The 1854 frame mansion depicts the life of a well-to-do estate owner of the mid-nineteenth century. The Rolfe-Warren House, a few miles off Route 10 near Surry, stands on a grant that was part of the Jamestown Colony and which was given to John Rolfe upon his marriage to Pocahontas.

The interior is handsome, not pretty, since it lacks the frills that came along later. Also along Route 10 are Bacon's Castle, that early bastion of freedom; Brandon; and Willow Hill.

Hopewell's modern environmental problems obscure its vital role in Tidewater. First known as City Point, it was the last port on the James and thus the way to the interior. Across its docks passed lumber and tobacco and the utensils badly needed on the frontier. Merchant's Hope Church, completed in 1657, is small, but the exterior brickwork has been cited as the most beautiful example of colonial handicrafts in America. Hopewell's most historic home, Appomattox Manor, has been owned by the Eppes family since 1655. Hopewell's strategic location made it a prime target during the Civil War; the remains of Fort Abbott are a good example of the earthworks used extensively during the war.

## The Virginia Peninsula

North of the James lies the Virginia Peninsula. History has favored this area in a unique way. The Historic Triangle—Jamestown, Williamsburg, and Yorktown—assembles as much history as any place of comparable size in America. Within a distance of twenty-five miles, the nation started, developed ideas and ideals that greatly influenced the American way of life, won independence and nationhood, and helped establish trans-oceanic relations that have been part of the national identity for more than two hundred years. The heroes of the Historic Triangle are the heroes of early American history: among them, Captain John Smith; the Indian maiden Pocahontas; Christopher Newport, the one-armed sea captain who kept the colony supplied; George Washington; Thomas Jefferson; James Madison; Comte de Rochambeau; Marquis de Lafayette; and Baron Von Steuben.

Virginians have not been content to restore and reconstruct this early period; they have recreated examples of the life-styles of the seventeenth and eighteenth centuries. The spectacles that delighted colonial audiences still exist at Colonial Williamsburg: fife and drum corps parade on Duke of Gloucester Street, soldiers fire flintlocks, halbardier guards drill, horse-drawn carriages amble along cobbled streets, and the sweet smell of colonial cuisine drifts from the kitchens of authentically restored King's Arms and Chowning's and Christiana Campbell's taverns. Candles, guns, wigs, stringed musical instruments, cabinets, and silver utensils are made just the way they were two hundred years ago. About one hundred people in Williamsburg earn their livelihood at colonial trades. And at Jamestown, replicas of the tiny ships that brought the settlers—the Susan Constant, the Godspeed, and the Discovery—ride at anchor off the wooden fort with its mud and wattle homes.

America's triangle of decision is connected by the Colonial National Parkway, one of the nation's first scenic routes. It passes through oak, pine, and flowering dogwood and has his-

Bacon's Castle Baptist Church **opposite** is named after one of the most prestigious of early plantations. Its owner fomented revolt a century before the American Revolution.

Visitors to Colonial Williamsburg **left** may ride in carriages, as their ancestors did, along authentically reconstructed streets.

Men dressed up to look like this **musket-bearing militiaman** are part of Williamsburg's colorful celebration of the colonial era.

In these tiny vessels sailed
the people who founded the nation. Full-scale
representations of the *Susan
Constant, Godspeed* and *Discovery* are part of
the presentation at Jamestown,
site of the first permanent English colony.

# JAMESTOWN'S RECONSTRU

The first Virginians constructed a triangle-shaped log fort, which has been reconstructed at Jamestown **above**. Attendants recreate the lifestyle of the founding settlement. Mud and wattle houses, church, and storehouses combined British building methods with local materials **left**.
This reconstructed kitchen **below left** is authentic in every detail, but the first settlers did not always have good enough to go around.
Household chores such as sewing **below** were vital when Americans lived in such an isolated colony. America's first industry was a glassworks now recreated at Jamestown **center**. Workers fashion crafts the way the nation's founding settlers did.

**T E D   F O R T**

The Indian maiden Pocahontas, remembered by this statue at Jamestown **left**, befriended the struggling colony, married John Rolfe, and lived in England until her death. To be descended from Pocahontas is a mark of distinction in Virginia.

toric and scenic turnouts overlooking the broad York and James rivers.

*Jamestown*

There are two parts to Jamestown: Jamestown Festival Park, constructed in 1957 for the three-hundred-and-fiftieth anniversary of the founding of the colony, and the national park, which preserves the archaeological remains of the actual site.

The early character of the colony, from the ships and mud and wattle homes to the Indian lodge patterned after that of Chief Powhatan, is recreated at Jamestown Festival Park. The

The colorful Fife and Drum Corps **above** and **below**, true in every detail to its colonial ancestor, participates in all official functions and holiday programs at Colonial Willamsburg.

Old World Pavilion depicts the many-sided relationship that developed between the Old World and the New during this period, with several historical scenes depicted in life-size dioramas. The fictions of the period are not forgotten; one tale to attract colonists told of streets paved with gold and semiprecious stones washed ashore on sandy beaches. The New World Pavilion shows the colony progressing in stature.

The national park preserves the ruins of the solid brick and frame community that grew up following the fort settlement. Excavation has revealed the foundations of the buildings, and thus most of the outline of the town. Paintings of the original buildings improve the presenta-

**Left** Colonial Williamsburg's two-week prelude to Independence celebration concludes with parades, demonstrations, and fireworks on the Fourth of July.

Captain John Smith **right** stares at the broad James River, much as he must have done in real life. Virginia's first colonial legend was created when Pocahontas saved the life of this professional soldier.

tion. The brick tower of the original church stands as a reminder of how solidly these settlers planted their colony. Statues of Captain John Smith and Pocahontas recall the most lasting legend of the colony, that of the Indian maiden who offered her own life to save that of the captain.

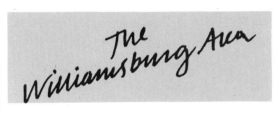

*The Williamsburg Area*

Colonial Williamsburg is planned diversity. Eighty-eight buildings have been restored, with two hundred rooms in forty-five of them furnished in colonial furniture and open for public viewing. Colonial Williamsburg has one of the finest collections of antiques in the United States. The following inscription sums up the philosophy that directs the not-for-profit foundation that operates it: "The appeals of Williamsburg are endless. Certainly, the most popular is the historical significance, but no list of appeals could overlook the architecture, the research programs, the crafts, the gardens, and the extensive collections." The foundation is dedicated to authenticity, and painstaking research goes into every project. The most recent restoration is the colonial hospital for the insane, which has been reconstructed on the original site.

Colonial Williamsburg is organized around Duke of Gloucester Street and the Palace green, just as was the colonial capital. Along Duke of Gloucester Street are the neat, frame buildings typical of the period: Raleigh Tavern, now an exhibition building; King's Arms, Williamsburg's most prestigious restaurant, with a menu featuring dishes based on colonial recipes; and crafts shops where milliners and silversmiths and others fashion wares the way their ancestors created them. The brick powder magazine, now a repository of antique guns, and historic Bruton Parish Church stand near the center of the famous street. At each end of Duke of Gloucester Street is a major public building: at the western end stands the Wren Building of the College of William and Mary, one of the finest products of the genius of Sir Christopher Wren; at the eastern end of the street is the functionally H-shaped Colonial Capitol, which, except for the taverns, witnessed more important Revolutionary discussion than any other place in the city. Visitors taking a conducted tour of the Capitol sit in seats of the original members of the House of Burgesses and hear discussions on some of the burning issues of the period. From this room, Richard Henry Lee rode to Philadelphia to introduce the Declaration of Independence so ably drafted by Thomas Jefferson. The Royal Council chamber, on the second floor, and the adjacent committee room also witnessed scenes of stirring and fateful debate.

The colonial governor's mansion is called the Governor's Palace, a name given to it by the contemporary public because of its high cost. Today's visitors will appreciate the extravagance because they will view one of the finest collections of English and American

A restored windmill in a
cornfield at Williamsburg serves as a
reminder that the workaday
life in Colonial times was hard, and that not
everyone lived in a mansion.

The symmetrical Colonial
Capitol was the seat of government both
before and during the Revolution.
The Virginia General Assembly, the oldest
legislative body in the Western
hemisphere meets in the reconstructed
building once every year.

The Powder Magazine, constructed in 1715 **above**, holds a display of the arms used during the Revolutionary period. In the Colonial period, the arms were the property of the citizens, who reacted angrily when the governor appointed by the king removed them to prevent revolt.

Raleigh Tavern **middle** was a center of social and political life before and during the Revolutionary War. George Washington and Thomas Jefferson both would feel at home in the authentically restored building.

antiques anywhere, as well as Spanish leather wallpaper, a harpsichord, Delft tiles, Italian marble, and a liberal amount of Chinese decorative influence. The English lion, Scottish unicorn, and the coat of arms of George III testify to the colony's strong bond to the British crown.

The Brush-Evarard House is a middle-class residence, built by a gunsmith, and it is shown as it was in 1750 when it served as the home of a city mayor. The George Wythe House, home of the law professor to Thomas Jefferson and other early legal minds, has a small garden that contrasts sharply with the formal plantings at the nearby Governor's Palace.

Carter's Grove, six miles from Williamsburg, stands at the end of a country road reminiscent of the elegant colonial estate's early days. The handsome Georgian mansion and formal garden are complemented by craftsmen and farmers re-creating activities that the untitled nobility of the young state would have witnessed. A reconstructed watchtower recalls an even earlier period, when the Woldstenholme Towne stood on the riverbank. The town, founded in 1619 and wiped out in the Indian massacre of 1622, was

The King's Arms **left** continues to dispense conviviality colonial-style as one of the period restaurants operated by the Colonial Williamsburg Foundation.

Costumed attendants **below** are commonplace in Williamsburg, where hosts and hostesses in display buildings, at festivals, and in gardens and restaurants recreate the eighteenth-century lifestyle.

The colonial Duke of Gloucester
Street in Williamsburg has been authentically
recreated, although some
buildings like these are privately owned and
not open to the public.

The eighteenth-century
emphasis on decorative gardens, large and
small, is recalled at Williamsburg.
This simple garden contrasts with the
extensive formal gardens
at the Governor's Palace.

The Governor's Palace in Williamsburg **right** and **center**, now restored, was described by a contemporary of its builder, Governor Spotswood, as "by far the most beautiful" public building in the colony. It is furnished with one of the finest collections of antiques in America.

Carter's Grove **below** is one of the magnificent mansions that wealthy planters built along the James River. This elegant hilltop structure, with terraces leading down to the river, was built by Carter Burwell, grandson of Robert "King" Carter. It is a splendid example of early Georgian architecture.

uncovered only in recent years by Williamsburg archaeologist Ivor Noel Hume.

Yorktown, the third point in the Historic Triangle, provides a classic example of the eighteenth-century style of conducting battles. The protective hornworks, redoubts prickly and abatis, and French and British cannon mounted on the main British line reveal how George Washington's ever-tightening siege lines forced the British commander, Lord Cornwallis, to surrender. The French connection is strong. At Redoubt 9, which French soldiers stormed and captured, The American Legion, composed of soldiers of all

Restored Colonial Williamsburg **left** presents a vivid picture of daily life in the 1700s. Here sheep are herded in front of the Governor's Palace.

Bruton Parish Church **below** was designed by Governor Spotswood but later became a divided center of revolt. Its bell was rung to announce all major community events, and graves hold some of the colony's elite.

Busch Gardens **above** near Williamsburg emphasizes America's ties with the "Old Country." Areas feature cultural experiences from Great Britain, France, Germany and Italy.

These French cannon **right** point across the Yorktown battlefield, where British forces under Lord Cornwallis surrendered in 1781. The victory guaranteed American independence.

wars since World War I, has placed a memorial "in commemoration of the French soldiers who gave their lives for American freedom." The so-called "Lafayette cannon" gets its name from an incident that happened long after the war; on a return trip to the United States, Lafayette identified it as one that had been surrendered to him by Cornwallis. The Victory Monument, authorized by Congress soon after the battle but not raised until a hundred years later, also recalls the importance of French forces in the decisive battle. The inscription reads: "At York on October 19, 1781, after a siege of 19 days by 5,500 American and 7,000 French troops of the line, 3,000 Virginia militia under command of General Thomas Nelson and 35 French ships of war, Earl Cornwallis, commander of the British forces at York and Gloucester, surrendered his army of 7,251 officers and men, 840 seamen, 244 cannon and 24 standards to His Excellency George Washington, commander-in-chief of the combined forces of America and France, to his Excellency, the Comte de Rochambeau, commanding the auxiliary troops of His Most Christian Majesty in

Victory at Yorktown was sweet, but this handsome monument **left** was a long time in coming. Although authorized by Congress soon after the battle, it was not erected until a century later.

**George Washington** was born on the family estate, later known as Wakefield, on the banks of the Potomac in Westmoreland county. The house in which he was born was destroyed by fire in 1779, but a reconstruction of it was raised on the original foundations in 1931.

John Tyler moved to Sherwood Forest **right** and **opposite**, with his young bride after he completed his term as president. He chose this name for his home, not far from his birthplace, because he considered himself a political outlaw. This dependency at Sherwood Forest indicates the simple life of even the gentry in the early period of American history.
The Smokehouse, **center**, was used for curing meat and fish.

America, and His Excellency, the Comte de Grasse, commander-in-chief of the naval army of France in Chesapeake."

At one point on Yorktown's Main Street, it is possible to see seven buildings that were there at the time Cornwallis surrendered. Among them are the brick Nelson House and the white frame Dudley Diggs House. The waterfront bears little resemblance to the thriving port that existed in 1781, when Cornwallis chose to encamp there. The Moore House, beyond the battlefield, has been restored to the condition in which it was when surrender terms were negotiated there.

*Plantations*

If there is such a thing as a royal road in America, it is the short State Route 5 between Williamsburg and Richmond. There lay great Tory plantations, whose owners dominated the colony and for whom independence was a negation of their English heritage. But the Tidewater barons had neighbors who were as American as apple pie. Two presidents of the United States, William H. Harrison and John Tyler, were born in Tidewater, within a distance of twenty-five miles of each other. The plantation houses that remain—Sherwood Forest, Berkeley, Shirley, and Westover— reflect the division of loyalties and difference in wealth. White frame Sherwood Forest, the home of President John Tyler and his young bride after he left the presidency, is not a typi-

cal plantation house, but more the pride of a well-to-do farmer. Tyler's individualism shows in the name he chose for the estate, which represents his own belief that he was a kind of political outlaw. Typically, he bolted the house's name so securely to the door that it remains there to this day. Sherwood Forest, only a few miles from Tyler's birthplace, was built in stages, beginning about 1730, and only the last stage was added by Tyler. The three-hundred-foot-long house—extensions were made end to end—remains pretty much as Tyler left it. The woodwork and plaster are original, and about two-thirds of the furnishings belonged to the tenth president, including some of his lawbooks, an extensive collection of mirrors, family portraits, china, porcelain, and a Boule clock made of ebony, brass, and semiprecious stones. A small hallway is hung with graphics of the Tyler period, among them a campaign poster for William Henry Harrison (nicknamed "Old Tippecanoe" for his exploits in the Northwest Territory) and Tyler, who became president upon Harrison's untimely death.

Despite Harrison's association with the frontier, he was actually born seventeen miles from Sherwood Forest, at Berkeley Plantation. The 1728 Georgian mansion, with terraced gardens leading down to the river, epitomizes what the well-housed plantation owner demanded in the early days of the nation. The plantation's roots go back well beyond that, however, to the founding of the colony. Harrison's Landing, on the riverfront at Berkeley, was the site of the first American Thanksgiving. The tradition began on December 4, 1619, when settlers stepped ashore from the "good ship Margaret" and "gave thanks for a safe journey." Berkeley Plantation was occupied by Union forces during the Peninsula

John Tyler, the tenth president,
had a wry sense of humor and a fondness for
dancing. He added a ballroom
at elongated Sherwood Forest.

Berkeley Plantation was
the home of the Harrison family, which
produced two presidents.
The farm and its occupants have been party
to many historic moments,
from the first Thanksgiving to Civil War
battles.

This Civil War cannon from the water battery at Fort Monroe **right** now faces the parade ground. The early nineteenth-century fort, one of a series authorized by Congress after the War of 1812, is still an active Army post. The casemate where Confederate President Jefferson Davis was imprisoned is now a museum.

**Previous page** Shirley is the tallest and one of the most handsome of James River colonial mansions. It has been owned by the same family since it was completed in 1760 as a wedding gift for Elizabeth Hill Carter.

campaign of the Civil War and helped inspire Brigadier General Daniel C. Butterfield to compose "Taps."

Harrison family portraits appear throughout the house, which is decorated in antiques of the colonial period. The 1700 Queen Anne secretary illustrates the passion for gambling that affected William Byrd of nearby Westover. He bet the secretary in a card game—and lost. The wall of one room bears the signature of Benjamin Harrison III, which probably resulted from an impulse while the room was under renovation. The Harrison family was active in politics, and many discussions took place in the homey surroundings of Berkeley. This was man's work in those days, so the room set aside for it had doors too narrow for the hoop skirts worn by the ladies.

The Byrd ancestral home at Westover is a bit more sedate than the colorful aristocrat who built it. The spacious front lawn has one-hundred-year-old tulip poplars, and a formal garden surrounds the gravesite of William Byrd II. Byrd, who served as president of the Crown Council in the colony, was such a believer in fundamental rights of the colony that the following was engraved on his 1744 tombstone: "The constant enemy of all exorbitant power and hearty friend to the liberties of his country." The dependencies of the main house include the old kitchen and a shed over a dry well, which was the entrance to Westover's escape tunnel to the riverbank when Indians came marauding.

Shirley Plantation, a scant five miles from Westover, has a longevity of family association that distinguishes it. It has survived time and tragedy, dissent and disapproval, to remain in the same family since its completion as a wedding gift for Elizabeth Hill Carter in 1760. Shirley stands tall and imposing on a high riverbank, abutted by a splendid set of dependencies that, together with the tree-lined driveway, generate a genuine plantation portrait of both the best and the unsavory sides of early American living. The manor house is the tallest on the James River and has a number of unusual features, including, in the main hall, a three-storey staircase that stands without visible means of support, and a water faucet near the fireplace in the living room (the water is pumped in from outside). Brass floor transoms used in the house were quite innovative for their time. The mansion is best known for its collection of English silver, including the large bowl from which Nestor, the prize racehorse of Charles Carter, drank wine after winning races, and the superb paneling and carvings made by eighteenth-century artisans.

Shirley's folktales are just as fascinating as the estate. Its owners were vigorous men who made lasting impressions on the life of the plantation, and women who made quieter, but no less significant, contributions. The guest bedroom, once a library, housed the infant Robert E. Lee, whose mother was a Carter, and the mansion's resident ghost, a short-time visitor from England. Medallions over the mantel memorialize Henry Clay and Daniel Webster, two early congressional giants. Furthermore, the relics of the tragic Robert Carter, a blockade runner during the Civil War who died after a fall on the farm, are housed in the room.

Shirley reveals the very human nature of the people who lived in the early days of the nation. The ancient hand-blown window panes bear scratches left by young ladies testing the diamonds in their engagement rings. The raucous ways of the gentlemen show in the decanters, whose tops are marked with easily-felt symbols. The gentlemen needed those in the evenings to separate the kinds of wine when the light faded after a full dinner—and perhaps after quite a few glasses. At Shirley, one can feel the vibrancy of the people who created the Tidewater region and who colored it red, white and blue.

The city of Hampton has participated in every period in American history. The Jamestown settlement built tiny Fort Algernourne there as an outpost. Hampton was burned during both the Revolutionary and the Civil wars, the latter by her residents to keep it from falling into Union hands. Old Point Comfort was picked as the site of one of the mid-nineteenth-century forts designed to prevent invasion of the East Coast. The first fatality of the Civil War, Henry Lawson Wyatt of North Carolina, was killed in an unimportant skirmish at Big Bethel. The Langley Laboratory of the National Advisory Committee for Aeronautics had a hand in designing the planes that created the air age; the NACA's successor, the National Aeronautics and Space Administration, sent the first astronaut team to Hampton to initiate the space age.

Hampton's violent history has obliterated many historic structures, but the ones that remain are first-class. Saint John's Episcopal Church, which dates from 1728, sits in a downtown area redeveloped in colonial style. Emancipation Oak, on the grounds of prestigious Hampton Institute, organized as a training school for freed slaves, symbolizes the city's preeminence in free education. The first free school in America was located there when Benjamin Syme willed two hundred acres of land to support a teacher who would "keep a free school." Moated Fort Monroe has been in continuous use as a military installation since it was finished in 1834 under the watchful eye of a young lieutenant of engineers named Robert E. Lee. A display in the Casemate Museum shows how the range of the fort's cannon increased with the improvement in artillery. The museum also has the small cell where Confederate President Jefferson Davis was imprisoned after the Civil War. Development of the museum was spearheaded by Dr. Chester D. Bradley, who moved to Hampton from Indiana in the 1950s and who became interested in the stories surrounding Davis's imprisonment. The fort is now the headquarters of the United States Army's Doctrine and Training Command.

Hampton also has an aerospace park, where jet planes and rockets are displayed; Syms-Eaton Museum, with a reconstructed Indian village of the type that existed when the first English settlers arrived; and the space museum at the NASA's Langley Laboratory.

An association with seafood has been a constant element in Hampton history. The city is one of the major seafood centers in Virginia, so much so that the nickname of the city's oldest high school team is "Crabbers."

**Thomas Jefferson**, a rich Virginia planter and slave-owner, was governor of the colony from 1779 to 1781.

Newport News

Newport News is an old place name, apparently deriving from an incident in the early days of the colony when Captain Christopher Newport was in command of ships supplying the Jamestown colony. The captain's arrival at that point, which was the site of a good well,

Richmond **right** was only the third state capital, but it cherishes its primary position in the state's political life. The city also is a center of banking and commerce.

apparently constituted Newport's Good News to the beleaguered colonists. The name had contracted to Newport News long before the city was chartered in 1896 as the eastern terminus of the Chesapeake and Ohio Railroad. Collis P. Huntington founded the Newport News shipyard a few years later and gave it a motto: "We will build good ships, at a profit if we can, at a loss if we must, but always good ships." The shipyard has been a major producer of naval, passenger, and commercial vessels since its founding. The giant aircraft carriers and nuclear submarines of today, the

passenger liners *America* and *United States* (the world's fastest passenger vessel ever) are a far cry from the first ship built at the yard, the tug *Dorothy*, which is now proudly displayed at the entrance to the shipyard. The shipyard is the largest single employer in the state of Virginia, with more than twenty-nine thousand employees.

Newport News has an unusual association with martial arts. The Victory Arch stands over the route that millions of men took to and from troopships during two world wars; the War Memorial Museum of Virginia contains thou-

The **Confederate ironclad**, the CSS *Virginia* (also known as the *Merrimack*), was converted from a sailing ship for service in the Civil War and fought against the USS *Monitor* in the world's first all-ironclad naval battle.

ing development in the United States. The Mariners Museum is one of the best museums of its type, with numerous scale models of ships constructed at Newport News and a collection of miniature models that have been admired by experts and novices alike.

Off Newport News Point was fought one of the most significant naval engagements of the Civil War. There, the first battle of ironclad warships matched the USS *Monitor* against the CSS *Virginia* (also known as the *Merrimack*). Neither vessel survived the war, but naval warfare would never be the same again.

The present city of Newport News was formed in 1957 by the consolidation of the old city and Warwick County to create a community covering about seventy square miles.

*Richmond*

The Richmond-Petersburg axis is officially part of the Tidewater region, but it is almost a distinct region—by preference as well as by design of history. Although the Richmond settlement at the falls of the James River was insignificant compared to the great plantations on the river and the delightful city of Williamsburg, it had an advantage that none of the others had—relative safety in time of war. Thus, it was a natural site for the state capital and, having once gotten it, Richmond never let it go. Having the capital would breed in the citizens a special affection for their city. That Richmond was the third place selected for the capital, and got it more or less by default, meant nothing; it became "the" capital. The years as capital of the Confederacy only confirmed that status. Petersburg has been closely associated with Richmond economically. The fall of Petersburg during the Civil War doomed Richmond.

The history of Richmond is one of steady growth despite adversity. Heavy manufacturing and tobacco companies were attracted to the city ahead of other areas, even the well-situated coastal cities. It was the state's

sands of relics from the wars of this century. At Fort Eustis, home of the army's Transportation Center, a museum traces the evolution of military movement and displays a number of interesting military vehicles, including a "flying saucer" which rode on an air cushion only a few feet off the ground. Newport News Park, better known for camping and its lake, preserves some of the earthworks built for a battle there during the Civil War. Hilton Village, constructed during World War I to house workers and still a desirable residential community, is the first government-built hous-

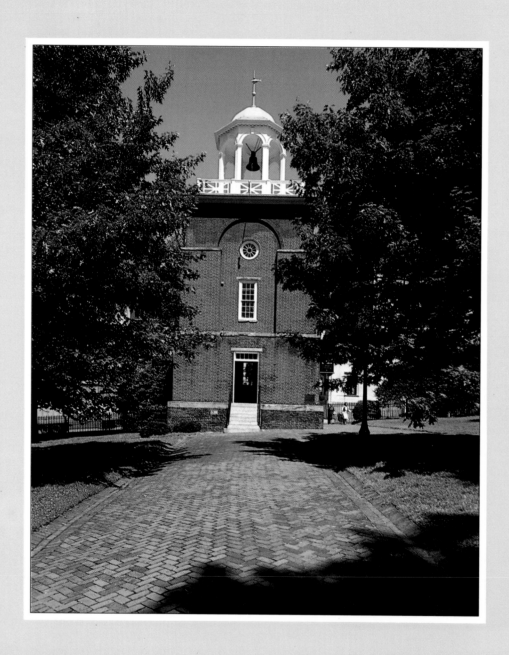

First used as a guardhouse,
this 1824 bell tower on the grounds of the
State Capitol in Richmond
now provides additional government office
space.

largest industrial center at the time of the Civil War, and contributed many of the heavy cannon used by Lee's Army of Northern Virginia. The failure of the Confederacy proved to be only a temporary setback. The city became the state's financial and managerial center, with Victorian iron-front buildings denoting solidity. The modern buildings within sight of Interstate 95 are the new wave of industrialization that crested during and after World War II.

Richmond burst across the James River to establish a suburban area that extends most of the twenty-three miles between Richmond and Petersburg. It has moved west and north as well, but not to the same extent. Broad Street is as much a description as a proper name, although this once-famous thoroughfare has deteriorated, as has much of the downtown area. Nevertheless, the traditional department stores, Miller and Rhoads and Thalhimer's, continue to buttress the area.

Richmond is unchallenged as the state's cultural leader. Its museums are superior. Its social life is more stratified than in any other area of the state; membership in the Commonwealth Club, Country Club of Virginia, and Saint Paul's Episcopal Church are the standards by which attainment is graded. Its colleges and universities are not among the most prestigious, but they train more students in more disciplines. The Medical College of Virginia, University of Richmond, Virginia Commonwealth University, and Union Theological Seminary are all considered superior. The state's best-known, most prestigious private high schools, Saint Catherine's, Saint Christopher's, and Collegiate, are located in Richmond.

Richmonders have class. They have seen war, hunger, fire, defeat, and occupation come and go and have survived them all without losing identity. They retain the memories they like, and discard the unpleasant ones. Richmond is not so staid as its old dowager image. Richmonders see nothing wrong with jokes about the equestrian statue of George Washington, which points to the place where the state penitentiary used to be. (Washington pointing the way for the members of the state legislature, the joke goes.) They are not surprised when one of them dismantles a fifteenth-century English manor house, Agecroft Hall, and transplants it in the West End. They revel in the resurrection, as a restaurant

This cast-iron building facade **left** is part of the outstanding heritage left by construction after the Civil War, and saved by conservationists from the modern building boom.

and shopping area, of a lusty waterfront section known as Shockoe Slip, which proper Richmonders would never have visited before. They accept their role as state leader with grace, and with the resignation that it is expected of them.

The white, columned State Capitol is one of the most famous, and most beautiful, buildings in Virginia. It was designed by Thomas Jefferson, who patterned it after the ancient Maison Carrée Roman Temple at Nîmes, France, but made some interesting modifications. The building has an unusual interior dome that provides a spectacular setting for Houdon's statue of George Washington. The building has been in regular use since its construction, and has witnessed more than its share of history. Aaron Burr was tried for treason there, and Robert E. Lee received his Confederate commission there. The Confederate Congress met there from 1862 until the end of the war. The nearby governor's mansion dates from 1812. Both Lee and Jefferson Davis worshipped at Saint Paul's Episcopal Church.

The **cast-iron façade** of this commercial building in Richmond bears witness to the city's confident growth as a financial center after the disruptions of the Civil War.

This monument in Capitol Square in Richmond **right** memorializes Virginia's contributions to the Revolutionary War. The equestrian statue of George Washington is attended by statues of other notable leaders of the period.

Shockoe Slip in Richmond **opposite**, once an industrial zone with an unsavory reputation, has been rejuvenated as a place of theme restaurants and chic shops.

Richmond's varied history makes it a good place in which to study architecture. The new glass and marble City Hall stands within a few blocks of the former Victorian stone one. Many of the iron fronts that certified the success of turn-of-the-century businesses have been saved despite downtown redevelopment. Among the most important buildings are the house constructed in 1790 by United States Supreme Court Justice John Marshall; the 1816 Confederate Museum, used as an office by Jefferson Davis during the Civil War; the Old Stone House, the oldest structure in the city and now a museum honoring author Edgar Allan Poe, who lived and wrote in Richmond; the 1812 Valentine Museum; the turn-of-the-century Jefferson Hotel, whose lobby once starred in a movie; the Egyptian Building at the Medical College; and neoclassical Broad Street Station, now a museum. Church Hill, in the eastern section of the city, has been designated a national historic landmark and is gradually being restored. The historic presentation is built around the 1844 Elmira Shelton home, where a young lady, one of Poe's friends, lived, and the white frame Saint John's Episcopal Church, where Patrick Henry delivered his famous "Give me liberty or give me death" speech. The original 1741 church is incorporated in the larger structure that stands today.

Richmond has a number of beautiful parks. Large William Byrd Park is a favorite, partly because of concerts at Dogwood Dell Amphitheater there, and the Carillon, a World War I memorial famous for its annual Christmas pageant. Maymont Park, with its small zoo and nature center, is naturally a favorite with children. A children's museum is located in the downtown area as well.

Hollywood Cemetery is the resting place of two presidents, John Tyler and James Monroe. The cast-iron tomb of Monroe, who was moved to this cemetery on the centennial of his birth in 1848, is considered one of the architectural monuments of the city. Also buried in the cemetery are three Confederate figures of note: Jefferson Davis and Generals J.E.B. Stuart and George E. Pickett. Matthew Fontaine Maury, known as the "Pathfinder of the Seas" for his work in oceanography, is also buried there.

Richmond was a frequent battleground during the Civil War, and the scars create a national military park along the eastern

perimeter of the city. The remnants vary from the Confederate earthworks at Chickahominy Bluff to the large earth redoubt known as Fort Harrison, and result from seven major attempts by Union forces to capture the city. At one point, the attacking Union army lost seven thousand men in a thirty-minute period, more than at any comparable time during the entire war.

Today's road pattern permits a convenient, fifty-seven-mile circular tour that starts at the visitors' center on Chimborazo Hill. Displays in the center explain the industrial and psychological importance of Richmond to the Confederacy and make more meaningful the numerous movements and shifting fortunes that created the battle sites. The two main areas are Cold Harbor, northeast of the city, and Fort Harrison. Cold Harbor is a drive-through park that preserves segments of earthworks raised by both armies, as well as the Gathright House, which served as a field hospital. Malvern Hill, between Cold Harbor and Fort Harrison, overlooks the rolling fields where attacking Confederate soldiers were decimated by concentrated Union fire. Fort Harrison, the largest and best preserved of the earthen forts, was divided into sections to minimize shell explosions. It was first an open-sided Confederate position and then a much stronger Union fort. In all the fighting, no point

Richmond's Church Hill neighborhood **left** has more than 300 restored townhouses from the eighteenth and nineteenth centuries, representing architectural styles ranging from Federal to late Victorian.

**Overleaf** Thomas Jefferson designed the State Capitol after the Maison Carrée in Nîmes, but added innovations such as an interior dome. The center was completed in 1788, and the wings were added in 1904. This was also the capitol of the Confederacy during the Civil War.

In St. John's Episcopal Church **opposite**, Patrick Henry delivered his "Give me liberty or give me death" speech. The smaller church that existed then is incorporated into the larger church that stands today.

The siege of Petersburg in 1864 sealed the fate of the Confederacy. The national historical park **above left** is one of the best-preserved Civil War battlefields and has many unusual features.

Arlington House, also known as the Custis-Lee House **above right**, is preserved as it was when Robert E. Lee made his decision to join the Confederacy. It overlooks the Potomac River and the national cemetery, which occupies the one-time plantation.

Church Hill, an historic section of Richmond **below**, is gradually being restored to its nineteenth-century appearance, when it was a favorite courting area for author Edgar Allen Poe.

was more important than a small, isolated outpost known as Fort Hoke. The Confederates who repulsed repeated Union attacks may, according to historians, have been the ones who did most to save Richmond.

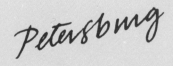

The battle switched to Petersburg, and the outcome was different. The ten-month siege of Petersburg broke the stubborn defence of the Confederate forces and caused the loss of Richmond. Within a few days, Lee surrendered at Appomattox, and, for all intents and purposes, the Civil War was over. The battlefield at Petersburg is among the best preserved and most instructive Civil War sites in the state. It includes the Crater, caused by an explosion in a five-hundred-foot tunnel dug by Union forces under a Confederate bastion. The park also has several miles of original earthworks, and representative cannon.

The glass walls of Richmond's
new City Hall refract the appearance of
nearby buildings, including
the stone Victorian structure that served until
the 1970s.

Old Blandford Church **above**, built in the 1730s, has witnessed both triumph and tragedy. British General William Phillips, killed in fighting near Petersburg during the Revolutionary War, was buried in the churchyard at night for fear of retaliation.

Downtown Richmond is architecturally eclectic, and somewhat jaded, but government and private sources are combining to modernize the area and preserve its historical structures **below**.

This stained glass window **opposite** is one of fifteen designed for the old Blanford Church by Louis C. Tiffany, one of the complete examples of his work still in existence. They were erected by

states to honor Revolutionary War dead. This one was placed by the state of North Carolina.

Petersburg's fame does not rest entirely on the Civil War battle. It was started as a frontier fort in 1645, and was burned during the Revolutionary War. British Major General William Phillips, killed in the fighting, was buried in Old Blandford Churchyard at night because of the fear of reprisal by local citizens. Old Blandford Church, built between 1734 and 1737, has fifteen Tiffany stained-glass windows. Petersburg was a regional commercial and tobacco center by 1850, when it was incorporated as a city.

The historic buildings in the downtown area chronicle the further history of the city. They include the 1817 Farmer's Bank, 1823 Center Hill mansion, the 1839 courthouse, 1842 Washington Street Methodist Church, and the nineteenth-century octagonal farmer's market.

Fort Lee, two miles east of Petersburg, shows off its importance as a quartermaster center at an on-base museum that depicts the supply side of the military, from the saddles used by General Ulysses S. Grant to the jeep used by World War II General George S. Patton. General Dwight David Eisenhower's wartime uniforms also are on display.

Lord Cornwallis looked at the stormy river and made a decision in desperation. He knew he could not continue to resist the tightening ring of American and French troops. For weeks, he had been penned against the York River at Yorktown, awaiting promised help by sea. It had been stopped by the fortuitous appearance of the French fleet off the Virginia capes. He knew that if he could get his army to Gloucester Point across the river, where he had placd a defensive outpost when he first came to Yorktown, he could fight his way north and escape the disgrace of surrender. The first boats moved slowly into the darkness of the river but soon became disorganized. Rain and wind literally drove them back to Yorktown.

This lost opportunity to escape defeat in 1781, Britain's last hope to retain its American colony, is symbolic of the way the Middle Peninsula remained outside the mainstream of Tidewater life most of its existence. Puny as Tidewater rivers go—the York actually is more an estuary of Chesapeake Bay than a river in its own right—it and its principal tributary, the Pamunkey River, effectively isolated the seven counties on the Middle Peninsula from the main currents of Tidewater development. In the colonial period, foreign sea captains had more contact with the residents of the Middle Peninsula than did their neighbors to the north and south. For the most part, the counties of Gloucester, Mathews, Middlesex, King and Queen, Caroline, Essex, and King William made do with what they had—farmland, timberlands, and waterways. The result was a pleasant, homespun parochialism, a clannishness, and an almost amoral shrewdness that persist to some extent to this day. Even after the Coleman Bridge replaced the ferry between Yorktown and Gloucester Point, it took a number of years before strangers entered, with complete confidence, the area of Gloucester known as "Guinea."

Agriculture and seafood fashioned the lifestyle of the Middle Peninsula for more than three hundred and fifty years. The singularity of the area ended with the land speculation that followed World War II. First came residents from nearby urban areas in search of summer homes. They were followed by retired industrialists and military officers. The foundations and land speculators were next, and unfamiliar names and accents began to float across Mobjack Bay, while roadside homes in Saluda advertised antiques and homemade products for passing drivers. Actors and actresses, real estate agents, and literary figures appeared, and even airline pilots opened stores as an avocation. This wave of people brought new prosperity to the area and initiated development that saw Gloucester Point become one of the fastest-growing areas in Tidewater.

*Gloucester County*

Gloucester County, always the leader of the Middle Peninsula, dates back to the earliest days of the Jamestown colony. A sizable number of farmers, attracted by the richness of the soil, the abundance and utility of the coves, and the striking beauty of the countryside settled there in the seventeenth century and remained despite an Indian massacre in 1644. The planters soon rivaled their cousins along the James in prestige, but not in political power. Gloucester was well enough developed by the eighteenth century to rank as one of the cultural centers of Tidewater. But Gloucester was not Williamsburg, with its fancy balls and boisterous taverns. Social activity took place at home, with neighbors riding over for the day and friends and relatives from distant farms staying overnight. Distance bred a fondness among relatives in Tidewater that has dissipated with the passage of time.

By 1690, population was spread out so much that Gloucester ceded one hundred square miles at the tip of the Middle Peninsula to form Mathews County. The steep-roofed Ware Episcopal Church, erected the same year, replaced an earlier structure that had served the parish since 1650. Abingdon Parish, also formed in 1650, waited until 1755 to build its present church structure. The parishes cooperated in operating a free school as early as 1675. The ruins of Rosewell, where, according to legend, Thomas Jefferson worked on the Declaration of Independence, prove the

The **belted kingfisher**, which nests in coastal and river banks, can easily be spotted on open water in winter by its tufted bushy crest and broad pale grey breastband.

**Opposite** Gloucester Courthouse, started in 1766, has received several additions over the centuries, the latest in 1956–57, and is still in use for its original purpose.

Many eighteenth- and
nineteenth-century private
homes are found in the
Gloucester County
Courthouse Square
historical district **right**.
Most of these homes are
privately owned and are
rarely open to the public.

wealth of the country gentry of the period.
Rosewell obviously was one of the most
elaborate homes in the Tidewater region.
Toddsbury Mansion was built in the 1658–60
period, but has been altered several times.
Long Bridge Ordinary, now owned by the
Gloucester Woman's Club, was erected in
1750 and later served as a stagecoach stop.

After its brief ascendancy during the
colonial period, Gloucester settled back into
relative obscurity. The county was more or
less an observer of the Revolutionary and Civil
wars. During the Union's ill-fated Peninsula
campaign against Richmond, Glostonians
could view the flotilla of federal naval vessels
from the shoreline and were visited by some of
the forces, but the fighting took place elsewhere. Farm produce went to market, fishermen went to sea and returned with a rich
harvest for the tables of Richmond, Washington, and points north. Dr. Walter Reed went
from rural Gloucester to Havana, Cuba, to dis-
cover the cause of yellow fever and to make
possible the digging of the Panama Canal.

U.S. Route 17, which traverses the peninsula from southeast to northwest, meanders
there like any good ribbon of history. History
is still being made at the Virginia Institute of
Marine Science, which is both a teaching and a
research institution. Founded in 1940, it trains
marine specialists and studies everything
from submerged vegetation to erosion and the
effects of pollutants. It cooperates with
researchers in other states on Chesapeake
Bay and with the federal government.

Gloucester Courthouse remains the center
of the county life. This government center is
also the primary market and cultural arbiter,
as well as a neutral meeting place for the
farmers and watermen, whose interests do not
always coincide. Grain, livestock, flowers, and
timber have replaced tobacco as the main
source of farm income. Flower-growing for
profit is a modern innovation. Daffodils are
now one of the county's best known crops,
and the bulbs are distributed nationally. In the
spring, thousands of residents of nearby areas
pour into Gloucester to witness the blooming
and to take home the yellow flowers they have
picked for themselves. A privately owned
Daffodil Mart Display Garden is located in the
Ware Neck area.

*The Urbanna Area*

Mathews County has experienced an
annual average growth of fewer than twelve
people since the first census was taken in
1800, and still has only eight thousand citizens. This condition is symptomatic of its
status as an appendage to Gloucester County.
But Mathews, wholly committed to the sea,
moves at an almost idyllic pace and has
attracted new settlers to offset the out-
migration of young people. Mathews fishermen continue to reap a rich harvest of oysters
and crabs from Chesapeake Bay.

Urbanna, on the Rappahannock River,
gained fame as a colonial port—and then lost
it. As a river port for the lucrative tobacco
trade, it was entitled to one of the twenty
tobacco warehouses authorized by the Virginia legislature in 1680. This expanded the
port and enriched the nearby plantations, but
Urbanna's commercial importance and
exposed position brought tragedy in every
major conflict. Privateers attacked Urbanna
and nearby plantations during the Revolutionary War; Union gunboats lobbed shells
ashore and at one point put troops ashore
during the Civil War.

Described in brochures as a "sleepy, historic river village," Urbanna provides a good
insight into the measured nature of life in the
late seventeenth century and early eighteenth

The Guinea area of
Gloucester County
**previous page** has
numerous small
communities associated
with the waterfront,
including Achilles, Severn
**88** and Maryus.

The **wild turkey**, much more streamlined than the domesticated fowl bred for eating, lives chiefly in forests and broken woodland.

century. It was one of the first places where land was purchased for a planned community, but growth was slow. The community did not have a proper name until 1705, when "ye towne lands" officially were renamed after the reigning British queen. Urbanna is literally the "city of Anne." Urbanna is seeking to make a major industry of its past. The colonial structures, including the old tobacco warehouse (now a library), are clustered in a small area in and around the town. The fiery Patrick Henry is supposed to have delivered a speech from the steps of the 1742 Old Tavern, and the 1750 Landsdowne mansion was a center of gracious living and lively debate. The old courthouse now houses the Middlesex Woman's Club, and the colonial Customs House, erected in 1695, is among the early remaining structures.

Three excellent examples of colonial country manors are located near Urbanna. Long, white Rosegill, built in 1675, was the victim of a great irony. During the Revolutionary War, patriots put the owner under restraint as a Tory; that did not keep a British privateer from plundering the mansion during the War of 1812. Hewick, raised in 1675, was a frequent gathering place of Urbanna's elite. Deerchase dates from 1700.

Historic Christ Church, a parish since 1666, is located a few miles from Urbanna. Christchurch School has a long tradition of providing quality education to the sons of "good" families. Nearby Saluda is noted for two things: the south campus of the Tidewater Community College and the retirement residence of the late Marine Corps General Lewis (Chesty) Puller. Both are recent develop-

ments. Tappahannock is an old community and has the relics to prove it, particularly the Old Jail. Tappahannock has been successful in attracting clean industries and, until the construction of the Grey's Point Bridge downriver, had the only fixed connection with the Northern Neck.

Essex County has a fascinating collection of old homes, all privately owned. Blandfield, built in the 1750–70 period by William Beverly, is still owned by his descendants. Book's Bank is even older, dating from 1731, and Elmwood has been restored to its original appearance after being considerably altered in the nineteenth century. Vauters Church is a good place to inspect the quality of early craftsmanship; it was built in two stages, in 1719 and in 1731, and the interior was altered in 1827.

Along the banks of the Mattaponi and Chickahominy rivers lie America's first Indian reservations, set aside for the survivors of the nine thousand Indians of the Powhatan Confederation who lived in Virginia when the English arrived. An estimated three thousand Indians, few of them of pure blood, live in the region now. Interest in their culture, which contributed words such as moccasin, hickory, terrapin, and hominy, has revived in recent years, along with recognition by whites of the contributions made by Indian society to the new colony. The colony may have survived because the settlers learned from the Indians to plant corn.

The Indian reservations do not differ substantially from other tiny rural communities in the region, except for small museums to interest tourists. The Mattaponi Pamunkey reservations are located on the Middle Peninsula. The tribes still pay an annual "tribute" of deer and turkeys to the Virginia governor, although this is now a promotional event rather than an actual obligation.

The town of West Point combines two elements in its name: It is the point at which the Mattaponi and Pamunkey rivers flow into the York; and it commemorates four West brothers, three of whom became governors of Virginia. It was settled in the early seventeenth century and became a port of entry in 1705. Its role as a railroad terminus gave it strategic importance in the Civil War, when it was attacked during the 1862 Peninsula Campaign against Richmond. Its principal industry is a paper mill.

**Overleaf** Christ Church in Kingston Parish, Mathews County, was built in 1908 to replace an older church that burned. The parish may be the oldest in the county. Captain Sallie Tompkins, the only woman to hold a commission in the Confederate army, is buried in the church cemetery.

**89**

# NORTHERN NECK

idewater's most remote peninsula, the Northern Neck, was not the most isolated. Captain John Smith explored the area around Coan River, actually little more than an estuary of the Potomac, and must have had some contact with the Pissaseck Indians, who already had well-established communities. The colonial history of the Northern Neck is spotted with the names of the great families of Virginia, especially the Carters, the Lees, and the Washingtons. As much leadership emanated from the counties of Lancaster, Westmoreland, Northumberland, Richmond, and King George and from the city of Fredericksburg as from any comparable area after the hegemony of the James ended. Westmoreland County gave birth to the Lees of the Revolutionary War—Richard Henry, Francis Lightfoot and Henry (Light-Horse Harry)—and to the Confederacy's most revered hero, Robert E. Lee. George Washington was born at Wakefield and grew up at Ferry Farm near Fredericksburg. James Monroe, the fifth president of the United States, whose proclamation of the Monroe Doctrine injected the United States into hemispheric affairs for all time, was born in Westmoreland County and practiced law in Fredericksburg.

No one had more influence on the Northern Neck than Robert "King" Carter, whose nickname derives from his temperament and the influence he possessed and wielded during the period when Virginia was emerging from the difficulties of settlement into the comfort of development. Carter was born in 1662, the son of an immigrant from England, and made his fortune as agent for Lord Fairfax, proprietor of all the land on the Northern Neck. In time, he became synonymous with the area. He was at various times treasurer of the Virginia colony, speaker of the House of Burgesses, a member of the Council, and acting governor of the colony from 1726 to 1727. He had two wives; the first died after eleven years of marriage, and the second died at age thirty-six. They gave him fifteen children, which may help account for the extraordinary number of Virginians who claim descent from Carter (probably second only to Pocahontas). Carter's progeny indeed were numerous and talented. Among them were eight governors of Virginia, three signers of the Declaration of Independence, two presidents of the United

States, a chief justice of the United States Supreme Court, a bishop of the Episcopal Church, and of course Robert E. Lee.

Life on the Northern Neck in colonial times was not easy; the landed gentry were not idle philosophers, but active overseers. Cultural life was limited; trend-setting Williamsburg was far away. The water produced finfish and shellfish to grace the tables, and the land produced vegetables for sustenance and, most of all, tobacco for trade. Off the ships came the cloth and kitchen utensils; onto the ships went the heavy hogsheads of tobacco. Like the rest of Virginia, the Northern Neck was officially Anglican, more tolerant in practice than the law allowed. Not all the dissenters were members of the lower and middle classes; some of them were landed gentry not afraid to press their cause of religious freedom. In Lancaster County, two Presbyterians notified the county court of their intention to establish a meeting hall for public worship, only to see the request rejected on the grounds it was contrary to the law. The Presbyterians won an appeal in the General Court and established a church.

The Northern Neck was isolated from the Revolutionary War but not from the War of 1812. The British burned a number of homes in the area as part of the devastation around Chesapeake Bay, but to a large extent the Northern Neck escaped the ravages of all save nature and accident. That may account for the large number of colonial homes that have survived. Shellfield, originally owned by a relative of George Washington, was built in 1656, and Epping Forest, birthplace of George Washington's mother, Mary Ball, was an active plantation in 1680. Most of the surviving homes date from the early part of the eighteenth century, attesting to a building boom in the period. "King" Carter raised Sabine Hall in 1720; the Lees established their ancestral keep, Stratford Hall, in 1725. Monrovia, birthplace of President Monroe, no longer exists, but was built in 1758. Nomini Church, erected in 1794, was burned by the British in 1814 and rebuilt in 1854. Yeocomico Church has been holding regular services since the seventeenth century. The present brick structure, with its T-shape, was raised in 1706 and restored in 1906.

Christ Church is the architectural gem of the area. It is beautifully preserved, partly

**Opposite** Mary Ball Washington, George's mother, lived in this Fredericksburg house until her death in 1789.

92

because it remained in the hands of the Carter family until 1960 and, thus, was not subject to periodic changes. It was financed by "King" Carter, and is cited in the Virginia Museum's 1968 survey of "Architecture in Virginia" as the "best preserved and most architectonic of Virginia's colonial churches." The family burial place of the first Carters in Virginia remains under the chancel, as "King" Carter insisted. The "King" and his two wives are buried in the churchyard.

## *Wakefield*

At Wakefield, where George Washington was born and played as a small boy, the traditional latchstring, signal to prospective visitors that they are welcome, is still out. The farm, with its restored farmhouse, is now a national monument operated by the National Park Service in a way that depicts both the Washington family life and the life-style of rising farmers of the early eighteenth century. Washington's great-grandfather, John, started the farm after emigrating from England about 1656. George's father was Augustine Washington.

Life was not easy for the Washingtons. The soil was rich, but harvests were not always bountiful. Practically everything that was used, from harness to hair ornaments, had to be produced on the farm, and the Washingtons were not slave-rich.

The handsome farmhouse is named the Memorial Building because it recreates a typical home of the period. The foundations of the Washington buildings have been excavated, but no plans remain of the house in which the first president was born, and which was destroyed by fire in 1799. The large central hallway extends from front to rear; this facilitated cooling and served as a dance hall on festive occasions. On one side of the hallway are the dining room and "withdrawing room," to which the ladies would repair after dinner. Both are furnished in antiques, and one table in the dining room is believed to have been

# SHINGTON'S BIRTHPLACE

George Washington was born on a plantation at Popes Creek, about 40 miles from Fredericksburg, in 1732. The original house burned down in 1776. The Memorial House at the George Washington Birthplace National Monument was built in 1932 **above left**, in the original style. The grounds have been restored to demonstrate a working plantation of the period **below right** and **left**. Farmers wear tricorn hats and colonial dress, and chat with visitors about the way things are done. Hosts and hostesses wear an odd kind of shoe that fits either foot and is made on the farm. This reconstruction **above right** is a typical farmhouse of the period.

Christ Church in Virginia's
Northern Neck is often regarded as the "best
preserved" of the state's
Colonial churches. It has changed little since
it was built by Robert "King"
Carter in 1732.

This H-shaped Georgian
mansion, the ancestral home of the Lees of
Virginia, was exceptional
in construction and design for a colony only a
hundred years old. It was
a center of Virginia political life, and Robert E.
Lee was born there.

This bedroom at Stratford **right** retains the appearance it had in 1800, when the house was remodeled by "Light Horse Harry" Lee. Other parts of the house are restored to their 1725 appearance.

owned by the Washingtons. The master bedroom and guest room are across the hall, and children's bedrooms are located on the second floor. The kitchen, which in good colonial fashion is separated from the main house, has a small museum containing archaeological finds and historical information about the Washingtons, as well as the usual cooking implements.

The future father of his country did not live at Wakefield long—the family moved to Ferry Farm near Fredericksburg while he was still a boy—but he remained a hard worker all his life and loved to ride among his fields, traits he may well have acquired at Wakefield.

Stratford Hall, with its unusual H-shape and handsome Georgian brick exterior, was built in 1725 on a twelve-hundred-acre Potomac River site by Thomas Lee, the first native-born Virginian to serve as governor of the state. The house was destined to become one of the most important places in the state. It became a state shrine in 1929 after it was purchased by the Robert E. Lee Memorial Foundation and meticulously restored to represent two periods. The library and two other rooms

The kitchen **left** was traditionally detached in Colonial homes as a precaution against fire. Stratford was no exception.

**Overleaf** This farm near Warsaw is typical of the rural atmosphere of Virginia's Northern Neck. Tourists are also discovering the area's historic atttractions and waterfront pleasures.

Tangier Island **right**, a two-by five-mile island in Chesapeake Bay, was settled by 1670, but remained isolated from the state for most of its existence. Descendants of the first settlers still live on the island.

*Tangier Island*

retain their original appearance; the room in which Robert E. Lee was born, the family parlor, and other family rooms are as they were remodeled by his father, Light-Horse Harry, around 1800. Seven of the twelve original outbuildings remain and have been incorporated into the restoration.

The Northern Neck, Fredericksburg excepted, depends on its farmland and waterways in much the same manner as does the Middle Peninsula. But the good fortune of conservation, the magic of restoration, and the proximity of the nation's capital and Baltimore have made tourism a rising industry. Tides Inn, one of the finest small resorts on the East Coast, is located at Irvington. The Chesapeake Bay steamboats that stopped at Irvington in the nineteenth century no longer are around, but patrons take the hotel's yacht for cruises on the nearby bay or rent pleasure craft from marinas at Hales Point, Sharps, Kinsale, Reedville, and other places. The beaches on the Potomac River at Westmoreland State Park, Potomac Beach and Colonial Beach are attractive, and, of course, the abundance of historical relics of many kinds is a potent reason for the tourist invasion.

From Reedville, a tour boat sails daily in the warm months to Tangier Island in Chesapeake Bay. Explored in 1608 by the peripatetic Captain John Smith and named after the North African city of the same name, the two-by-five-mile island received its first families in 1670. Their descendants constitute much of the population of the island today. This small island was so isolated through the centuries that the language spoken by the inhabitants, even in the early decades of the twentieth century, was closer to Elizabethan than to modern English. That has changed, but the islanders continue to live by the sea the way they have since their ancestors came. The soft-shell crabs from the island are considered delicacies, and food is served family-style to visitors.

Even though it has been discovered by tourists and now has a regular mailboat con-

Colonel Fielding Lewis risked beautiful Kenmore in Fredericksburg **left** to help pay for cannons for George Washington's army. The symmetry of the building and its interior design make it one of the most beautiful of the period.

nection to the Delmarva peninsula, Tangier Island retains the charm of semi-isolation. The nights are quiet, except for the lapping of the waves and the cries of seagulls. Islanders meet in the evenings to talk because there are no movies, no department stores. Life moves at a moderate pace during the day, as well; and since there are no automobiles, people are unencumbered by the noise and the smoke of engines. Islanders do their own thing, while the visitors wander the narrow lanes and visit the local museum or Methodist Church. Islanders do not make a fuss over visitors; they address them in the same frank way they talk to one another. The visitor soon realizes that Tangier remains its own island, no matter what comes.

*Fredericksburg*

Northern Neckers sometimes do not consider Fredericksburg to be part of their special little world, but the geographic and historic ties are too strong to be denied. Fredericksburg, one of the nation's most historic cities, revels in its own accomplishments. Remembrance focuses on two periods: the colonial–Revolutionary War period and the Civil War. Fredericksburg deserves the first because of its associations with the great man of the period; it was dealt with more directly, and more harshly, by the second.

The city of Fredericksburg, with fifteen thousand people easily the largest community in the area, began in 1676 as a fort protecting the port at the "falls" of the Rappahannock River. The city was officially founded and named in 1727, and it soon became a way station on the north-south land route between Richmond and Northern Virginia. Contact with its neighbors on the Northern Neck was direct and continuous. Ferry Farm, where George Washington went with his family as a small boy, is supposedly the site of the famous, but probably fabricated, cherry-tree story. The farm, now a park, also was the place from which Washington threw a dollar across the river. Whatever he threw, if anything, it wasn't a dollar, which was not even in use at the time

Hugh Mercer's Apothecary
Shop in Fredericksburg was more than a
dispensary of medicines.
Mercer's interest in American freedom no
doubt led to interesting
conversations with his customers. He joined
the army and died in the
Battle of Princeton. The office Washington
used when in town is on
display, along with scores of curious bottles
and antique showcases.

George Washington's brother Charles operated the Rising Sun Tavern **left** in Fredericksburg, built in 1760. Many Revolutionary War plots were discussed here **right**.

the event is supposed to have occurred. Another Fredericksburg tradition, the annual Dog Mart, is historically authenticated. It began in 1698 as a peacemaking gesture between the settlers and the Indians, on the theory that those who trade together, do not fight—at least, all the time. That remained just a theory in Fredericksburg, as it did throughout the colony. Intermittent warring and trading went on.

Downtown Fredericksburg has a number of well-preserved colonial buildings, the best of which is Kenmore. Built in 1752 on a flax and tobacco plantation of 863 acres, the red-brick mansion has great symmetry, with proportional windows and chimneys at each corner and an interior mantel depicting Aesop's fables. The owner, Colonel Fielding Lewis, was a generous financial backer of his brother-in-law, George Washington, during the Revolutionary War. He is sometimes called the "first apostle of national defense" because he traveled extensively to promote support of the continental forces. He used his own money to keep the Fredericksburg arms factory open and kept Washington's beleaguered army

supplied with muskets. Some historians believe the war might have been lost without his generosity. He paid dearly for it, and lost Kenmore as a result.

A white frame house on Charles Street was purchased in 1772 by George Washington for his mother, and she lived there until her death in 1789. Washington visited her on his ride to New York to be inaugurated as the first President of the nation. Mary Ball Washington's grave in Fredericksburg is topped by a slender marble obelisk that was dedicated in 1894 by President Grover Cleveland.

Fredericksburg has a good collection of colonial business and professional buildings. James Monroe practiced law from an office he built in 1786, now a museum and library. The desk on which he signed the Monroe Doctrine is there, along with a number of personal and state effects from his years in the White House. Rising Sun Tavern was built in 1760 by Charles, George Washington's brother, and was as much a favorite meeting place of early patriots as were other taverns in the state. The neat frame building is now a national landmark. Dr. Hugh Mercer, perhaps as well known a patriot as he was a doctor, operated the Apothecary Shop, now restored to its original appearance. Mercer was a native of Scotland, as were many of the people who settled in Fredericksburg.

Fredericksburg's second date with destiny came thirteen days before Christmas in 1862, when the Union army under the command of General Ambrose Burnside tried to drive out a smaller army commanded by General Lee. The battle is a classic study in attack and defense. More than 220,000 men were involved, and battle casualties in three days of fighting numbered almost 18,000. Of these,

Fredericksburg, on the route from Washington to the Confederate capital of Richmond, changed hands seven times during the Civil war. The national cemetery at Marye's Heights **right** contains the graves of more than 15,000 Union soldiers.

12,653 were the Union troops who tried repeatedly to force Lee from Marye's Heights south of the city. Names like Sunken Road and Stone Wall, physical features that influenced the outcome, became curse words on the lips of the attacking federals. The battlefield, including the steep slope of Marye's Heights, is preserved as a national military park and cemetery. The battle of Fredericksburg initiated a series of campaigns that would take place the next year in the Piedmont region, interrupted only by Lee's invasion of Pennsylvania and his damaging defeat at Gettysburg.

After the war, Fredericksburg remained an important center on the Richmond, Fredericksburg, and Potomac Railway line. It was a workaday job, but it was steady, because the RF & P is the shortest rail link between the northeast and the railroads in the south Atlantic region of the country. Stoner's Store suggests the pedestrian nature of the period; the nineteenth-century relic holds thirteen thousand items of Americana, from a baby buggy to high button shoes.

Fredericksburg's role as a transportation hub increased with the completion of Interstate 95, which skirts the western part of the city. This has led to considerable commercial development, including hotels and restaurants. Route 17, which meanders across much of Tidewater, intersects I-95 at Fredericksburg.

One of the city's newest attractions is located on the eastern edge of the city, however. Shannon Air Museum, at the city's small airport, owns fifteen antique aircraft, about half of them airworthy. The museum is named for a former vice president of Eastern Airlines, Sidney Shannon, Jr., and holds his trophies and personal artifacts.

One of Virginia's ablest Civil War commanders, General Thomas J. "Stonewall" Jackson, was fatally wounded at the Battle of Chancellorsville, near this monument **above**. Jackson died at a nearby farm, also a shrine.

The Confederate Cemetary **left** at Fredericksburg, on Marye's Height, one of the major fighting areas in the Battle of Fredericksburg, provides an inadequate concept of the carnage. Three days of fighting produced 18,000 casualties.

The map in the Arlington Historical Society's history of the county is an unusual one. It is oriented east-west, instead of north-south, and it has Arlington in a central position. That is understandable, considering the subject, but is a reversal of the county's historical role. For most of the 377 years of Virginia's history, Arlington was virtually ignored. Everybody knew it was there, but nobody thought much about it.

In a sense, that attitude has prevailed in Virginia toward most of what is today known as Northern Virginia, an ill-defined area that lies across the Potomac River from the nation's capital. In this area, the Tidewater region was narrow because the falls of the Potomac were located just northwest of the District of Columbia and the land was sparsely settled. What is today Arlington County was ceded to the federal government to help create the District of Columbia, only to be returned later to the state. At the time, if records of the period are accurate, only eight hundred people lived in the county . Except for Alexandria, which developed as an early colonial port, Northern Virginia remained the tag end of Tidewater through most of its existence. It was never really a part of the Confederacy because Union forces either occupied or dominated it throughout the war. Fort Ward in Alexandria, now in part restored to its Civil War appearance, formed part of the ring of defense protecting the national capital.

Northern Virginia, again save Alexandria, came into its own during and after World War II. The explosion in government, and in those businesses that depend on government, burst the boundaries of the nation's capital and spilled out into adjacent Virginia and Maryland. This changed the area forever and gave it a distinctive character from the rest of Tidewater—and the state as a whole. Northern Virginia has relatively few natives among its population; any group of a few people will reveal a variety of accents, few of them Virginian. The percentage of foreign-born in the population is higher in Northern Virginia than in any part of the state, including the ports around Hampton Roads. A high proportion of the residents obtain their livelihood from the nation's capital, although this has been decreasing a little ech year.

Alexandria, which remained aloof to its neighbors through the years, now is oriented toward Washington more than ever before. The other areas, which grew rapidly by providing bedrooms for people working in Washington, are developing their own business base in light manufacturing and services. That trend became obvious by the 1970s and may accelerate because of an influx of high-tech industry into the area. That does not mean that it has cut the umbilical cord to Washington; much of the financing of those expensive operations still comes from government salaries.

What is traditionally thought of as Northern Virginia—the Washington suburbs south of the Potomac—is now an urban area with attendant conditions, particularly clogged highways, heterogenous population, social problems, eclectic appearance, and lack of community identification. The multiplicity of governmental units makes administration and problem-solving difficult. Despite the heavy expenditures on Interstate 95 and the Beltway, traffic jams are common, especially during commuting hours. Northern Virginia moves at a much more rapid pace than any other part of the state. The area is expanding year by year, and suburban development already is reaching out into the Piedmont region.

*Alexandria*

Northern Virginia traces its origins to Alexandria, and Alexandria remains the part of Northern Virginia most closely allied with Tidewater. It has the same roots, and the same fierce pride in them. It is one of the most fascinating cities in Virginia because of its history as a colonial port, its associations with George Washington and Robert E. Lee, its well-preserved and carefully restored colonial section, and its towering Masonic memorial. The historic area in Alexandria is so compact that most people can easily follow a walking tour outlined by the Alexandria Tourist Council. Fort Ward and the Masonic Memorial are in other parts of the city.

**Opposite** The Great Falls of the Potomac tumble among irregular palisades 15 miles from the nation's capital of Washington, D.C. Virginia's great coastal and inland waterways offer many other spectacular sights.

The 333-foot-high Washington Masonic Memorial, which stands on Shooters Hill, is an unmistakable Alexandria landmark **opposite**. Its observation deck affords an impressive view of the city and countryside.

Gadsby's Tavern **above**, the center of male social life during the Revolution, still is used for important social events in Alexandria. Washington made his final appearance in military uniform there.

Alexandria **below** was occupied by the Union army for most of the Civil War, and therefore avoided much of the destruction that leveled many other towns in Virginia. Today, the citizens take pride in preserving the unusually large number of eighteenth- and early nineteenth-century buildings.

"A lively tradition" is how Alexandria sometimes styles itself, and the description is more than an idle boast. The city's heroes in the early years were neither pallid nor saints—they were as boisterous as the period in which they lived. Gadsby's Tavern, now restored, was the center of male social life. Merchants from the port talked business and patriots discussed revolution over a mug of ale. Washington knew the tavern well, and made his final appearance in military uniform there. The stories associated with the old tavern include a "female stranger" who was ill when she arrived on a ship and who died in a room of the tavern. Her name still is unknown.

Alexandria still uses Gadsby's Tavern for social events. The ballroom has been restored to its original appearance, and the colonial atmosphere has been preserved. The downtown area near Gadsby's has been developed in colonial style, and numerous historic structures have been preserved. It is the scene each year of several public events, including the annual Scottish Christmas Walk. Washington's former club, now the Old Club Inn, is one of seventy restaurants in the city's center. Alexandria's original Scottish inhabitants are

remembered in other ways, especially at the Old Presbyterian Meeting House on Fairfax Street. Still an active church, the present building was built in 1835 after its 1774 predecessor was gutted by fire. The outside walls were saved and incorporated in the reconstruction, so that the original exterior appearance was preserved. The small churchyard holds some of the lesser-known, but important, figures of the Revolutionary War, including Dr. James Craik, surgeon general of Washington's army, and the Unknown Soldier of the Revolution.

Of the many stories about this unknown soldier's grave, one proves that Alexandria was not a latecomer to ecumenical relations. The incident that brought this about was construction of the Roman Catholic chapel, now St. Mary's Church, adjacent to the grounds of the Meeting House. While digging the foundation for a wall, workmen, without realizing it, encroached upon the property of the Presbyterians. Being proper Scotsmen, elders of the church met to discuss the loss, even though it involved only a sliver of land. The result was duly recorded in the January 1821 minutes of the Session of the church as follows; "As our Catholic brethren have more use for that little piece of ground than we have, it is not proposed to make any objections."

The Session minutes also contain another entry that is significant, the reburial at the same time of "an old Revolutionary soldier from Kentucky." The digging of the chapel foundation had unearthed an old ammunition box that held the body of an unidentified soldier. The grave was simply moved a few feet and the body reinterred.

Neither of these events attracted public attention at the time. But nearly a century later, the old soldier emerged from obscurity. In 1926, while planning restoration work at the Presbyterian Meeting House, a woman recalled the significance of the. grave. Her father had pointed it out to her when she was a child and, to please him, she had from time to time placed flowers on the grave. Now, she proposed a permanent memorial. American Legion Post No. 24 placed a temporary marker; later, the National Society, Children of the American Revolution, provided the permanent marble monument that stands over the grave. The inscription is particularly fitting: "Here lies a soldier of the Revolution whose identity is known but to God. His was an ideal-

The Old Presbyterian Meeting Hall **center** is one of Alexandria's most historic churches. The Unknown Soldier of the American Revolution rests in the church cemetery, alongside several well-known leaders of the Revolution.

Carlyle House **left**, now restored to its 1750s appearance, hosted General Edward Braddock during the French and Indian Wars. It depicts how a rich merchant lived in the mid-eighteenth century.

ism that recognized a Supreme Being, that planted religious liberty on our shores, that overthrew despotism, that established a people's government, that wrote a Constitution setting metes and bounds of delegated authority, that fixed a standard of value upon men above gold and lifted high the torch of civil liberty along the pathway of mankind. In ourselves, his soul exists as part of ours, his memory's mansion."

Christ Episcopal Church, in keeping with Virginia tradition, is Alexandra's most historic church. It is practically unchanged from the time when George Washington worshipped there, sitting not far from a cut-glass chandelier that represented the best kind of lighting fixture available in the eighteenth century. The church was built in two stages, from 1767 to 1773, because the original contractor could not finish the building. The walled churchyard around the cheerful red-brick building with a domed steeple is an oasis from the busy life in the downtown area.

Alexandria began as a commercial center when a Scottish immigrant built a tobacco warehouse, and that side has always been close to the community's heart. Alexandria

Alexandria's first lord mayor lived in this unpretentious house **above** 250 years ago. The oldest house in the city, it now is used as a visitors center by the Alexandria Tourist Council.

Captain's Walk on Prince Street **right** recalls a time when Alexandria rivaled New York and Boston as a port for trade with the mother country.

This engraving shows a **horse-drawn fire-wagon** typical of the 18th century. Models of a similar design are displayed at the Morven Park museum of carriages, near Leesburg.

displays a record of that heritage with pride. The 250-year-old Ramsay House, now the home of the Alexandria Tourist Council, was originally the home of the city's first lord mayor. This structure, the oldest in the city, was moved to its present site in 1749. Carlyle House is more pretentious, and stands now just as it did in the 1750s when British General Edward Braddock stayed there. Wise Tavern is another early eighteenth-century structure.

Alexandria gained its early reputation as a port. During the colonial period, it was more important than either New York or Boston. At the time, it laid claim to being the third largest port in the New World, but decline set in after the Revolutionary War. The Old Port is alive again after a long period of neglect, as both a residential and a shopping area. One-block-long Captain's Walk on Price Street still has cobblestones, and South Fairfax and South

Lee streets look much as they did in colonial days. New port facilities are once again opening Alexandria to oceangoing vessels.

Washington's interest in Alexandria caused him to become a benefactor to Friendship Veterans Fire Company on South Alfred Street. The small, hand-operated pump engine displayed there was donated by Washington; it is part of a collection that also includes fire helmets from the eighteenth and nineteenth centuries and two early nineteenth-century engines. The Stabler-Leadbeater Apothecary Shop exemplifies the best in medicine preparation in the Revolutionary period.

Although Alexandria was Washington's 'home town," it served for a time as the home of another Virginian of great stature. Robert E. Lee spent his boyhood there, in a home on Oronoco Street, which was saved from destruction a few years ago by the Stonewall Jackson Memorial.

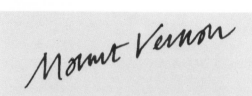

Mount Vernon, nine miles from Alexandria, could not provide a more perfect picture if it were a painting. The columned white mansion sits on a knoll that slopes gently down to the broad Potomic River. The beautifully proportioned house, started probably in the 1735-39 period by George's father, Augustine, harmonizes with the setting. It is easy to understand why George Washington loved this plantation above all places. Sitting in a rocking chair on the porch, one is struck by one of the greatest ironies of George's life, that he was forced by duty to spend so much time away from home and family, the two things he loved most. Mount Vernon reflects Washington's preferences in style and decoration, as well as the life-style of the mid-eighteenth century. The interior is handsome, not ornate, and the antiques reflect the tastes of a plantation owner. The grounds and dependencies are a good representation of plantation living. The gardens contain the mixture of flowers and shrubs typical of the period, and are complete

Hundreds of old bottles
are the major attraction at the
Stabler-Leadbetter Apothecary
in Alexandria. George Washington, Robert E.
Lee, and Daniel Webster
were among the patrons.

The striking beauty of Mount Vernon **opposite** suggests why George Washington loved this place above all others. Although duty often took him away from the plantation, he died there and is buried near the mansion.

The gardens at Mount Vernon **above** have been replanted the way Washington designed them, even down to an experimental garden where he spent considerable time.

Robert E. Lee spent two periods of his youth in this house **left**, which is noted for its central hallway and woodwork. It recreates a home in the first half of the nineteenth century.

even to the experimental botanical garden that George is known to have planted.

Restoration of Mount Vernon was a pioneering effort by one of the first ladies' organizations created for such a purpose. The property was acquired in 1858 by the newly-formed Mount Vernon Ladies Association, which saved the house from certain destruction. Restoration of both the mansion and the numerous dependencies has been a continuing process since.

Washington died at Mount Vernon in 1799 after catching cold on a ride around his fields; he is buried in the place he selected as a family burial ground. The marble sarcophagus and brick crypt were added later.

The home of another patriot, whom Washington admired as one of the "strongest intellects" of his time, is also near Alexandria. Gunston Hall, the home of George Mason, is known for the beauty of its formal gardens, but also is an excellent example of mid-eighteenth-century Georgian architecture. Mason was author of the Virginian Declaration of Rights of 1776, which became the basis for the federal Bill of Rights, and he was one of the framers of the Constitution.

*Fairfax County*

Pohick Church, twelve miles from Alexandria in Fairfax County, is one of several churches constructed by a vestry that included George Washington and George Mason. The 1769–74 church makes extensive use of stone in its red-brick design. The exterior has changed little through the years, but the interior was stripped during the Civil War and has been restored twice since then.

Fort Belvoir occupies the site of a historic plantation and presently is the home of the United States Army's engineering school and museum. The museum traces the two-hundred-year history of that branch of the service.

Fairfax County has a split personality. The northern end is part of the Washington suburbs, while the southern end retains some of its former rural charm. The county is divided into numerous communities, the names of which are clues to their ancestry. Fairfax

117

**Fairfax courthouse**, shown during the Civil War, was built in 1799 and restored in 1967. It houses the wills of George and Martha Washington.

recalls the noble land speculator whose land holdings were enormous. Falls Church gets its name from the construction of a church not far from the falls of the Potomac. Occoquan is an Indian word meaning "end of the water."

In the 1800 Fairfax Courthouse are the wills of George and Martha Washington. Falls Church, erected in 1769, is a plain brick structure whose simplicity is appealing; it was one of those built by the vestry on which George Washington served. West of Fairfax, on U.S. Routes 29 and 211, are the gardens and fountains of the National Memorial Park. The thirty-three figures of the Fountain of Faith were designed by Swedish sculptor Carl Milles. Another sculpture commemorates a World War II incident in which Protestant, Catholic and Jewish chaplains aboard the torpedoed troopship *Dorchester* gave their life jackets to others and sang "Nearer My God To Thee" as the ship sank.

## Arlington County

Arlington County was known to the early settlers of Virginia as part of Alexandria County, but was sparsely settled and remained an adjunct to the city of Alexandria. At the time of the Revolutionary War, only eight hundred people resided there. It was given away twice; Virginia ceded it to the federal government as part of the District of Columbia, and the federal government gave it back when all the early development took place on the opposite shore of the Potomac River. Federal troops occupied the area throughout the Civil War, in order to protect the approaches to Washington; this naturally did not encourage growth and development. In 1870, when a new Virginia constitution separated counties and cities, Arlington and Alexandria, which together had formed Alexandria County, went their separate ways. Arlington had thirty-one hundred citizens at the time, and did not begin to grow until the turn of the century. The period of great population growth, which still is going on, began in the 1930s with the expan-

Arlington National Cemetery **center** was created in 1864. Among the many noted American military heroes buried here are Admiral Robert E. Peary, General John J. Pershing, Admiral Richard E. Byrd and General George C. Marshall.

The "Old Guard" maintains a 24-hour watch **left** at the Tomb of the Unknown Soldier in Arlington National Cemetery, where remains beginning with World War I are buried. The guard is changed every half-hour. The soldiers wear Colonial garb on special occasions.

sion of the role of the federal government. The period of greatest expansion was during and since World War II. In the decade of the 1940s, farmlands began to disappear under residential subdivisions, shopping centers, high-rise apartments, and superhighways.

Arlington's most famous sights are related to the military. The Pentagon, a twenty-nine-acre structure across the Potomac from downtown Washington, is the nerve center of the worldwide commitments of the American armed services. Visitors may take a guided tour of the confusing corridors (there are many stories of visitors who became lost for years and came out as colonels) and watch a film presentation.

*Arlington National Cemetery*

Arlington's most popular attraction is the national cemetery, also just across the river from the national capital. It is the site of the marble Tomb of the Unknown Soldier, which

**Overleaf** A famous World War II incident is depicted by the floodlit Iwo Jima Monument in Arlington National Cemetery. The Washington and Lincoln memorials are visible in the background. **119**

Arlington House is
maintained to reflect the
distinguished past.

The Great Falls of the Potomac **above** tumble among irregular palisades 15 miles from the nation's capital of Washington, D.C. Virginia's great coastal and inland waterways offer many other spectacular sights.

The grave of assassinated President John F. Kennedy **below** is one of the most visited places in Arlington National Cemetery. It occupies a hillside site facing the nation's capital.

honors the dead of all services in all wars since World War I. The guards, who march silently in measured steps before the tomb, are from the Old Guard, the First Battalion of the Third Infantry Regiment. The guards wear Revolutionary War uniforms for special parade occasions. Two martyred presidents are buried in the cemetery.

The grave of President John F. Kennedy, assassinated in 1963, is topped by an eternal flame. The gravesite of another president, William Howard Taft, is marked by a simpler memorial. Pierre L'Enfant, who designed the city of Washington, also is buried in the cemetery.

The cemetery originally was a plantation where both Robert E. Lee and George Washington Parke Custis, grandson of Martha Washington, lived for a time. The mansion, from which Arlington County took its name, is one of the most beautiful in the area. It is furnished in period style and is a nostalgic treat for visitors.

In Northern Virginia, Tidewater ends at the Great Falls of the Potomac. This sizable obstacle to navigation was circumvented by a canal, whose locks are now an open air museum. The paths of the park are popular with joggers.

# PIEDMONT

The Virginia Piedmont is a classic example of this topographic feature. It ascends gently from the coastal plain of the Tidewater to the Alleghenies, rising to about one thousand feet at the base of the mountains. The land is not flat, but undulating, with definite terrain features. The region drains two ways: to the Tidewater Virginia region and to eastern North Carolina, the latter giving part of the Virginia Piedmont a special orientation toward that adjacent state. The headwaters and tributaries of some of the great Tidewater rivers traverse the piedmont. The mighty James stretches all the way to the mountains. The Potomac divides and subdivides far back into West Virginia. The Rappahannock gathers its first waters in the Piedmont, and the tributaries of the York River drain the central portion of the region. These rivers have had a major impact on the area. So have their tributaries—the Rapidan, North Anna, South Anna, Appomattox—which, although tributaries, are major streams in their own right. The Roanoke River flows into North Carolina, and the history of the river basin is tied as much to that state as to Virginia.

The Piedmont region, one hundred and sixty miles wide at its base on the North Carolina boundary and forty miles wide in the north, has a respectable sprinkling of industries but is predominately agricultural. The agriculture divides roughly into two categories: south of Interstate 64, which connects Richmond and Charlottesville, are tobacco crops; north of the highway are grain fields and grazing areas, including those in Orange and Loudoun counties, famous for breeding fine show horses. Except in the far north, where the influence of Washington is beginning to be felt, the urban areas in the Piedmont are market towns or transportation hubs.

Virginia's Piedmont is as English in origin as is the Tidewater. Most of the place names are taken either from the mother country, such as Buckingham, Brunswick, and Culpepper, or like Lynchburg, from individuals who first settled there. The people of the Piedmont are quite different in outlook from those in the Tidewater. Patrick Henry's tough words arose from his Piedmont background. When he defended dissenters in the courts of Virginia, dominated by the Anglican Church, he was defending the less conformist style that had developed in the Piedmont. Many of his acquaintances were dissenters, and he saw no reason to fear them. Living standards were much simpler in the Piedmont; Patrick Henry's home, Scotchtown, clearly shows that. Few cultural institutions matched those in the Tidewater region. The Piedmont was as devoted to education as the other areas of Virginia, however; Hampden-Sydney College, the University of Virginia, Randolph-Macon College, Longwood, Sweet Briar and others have fine traditions of excellent education. Neither did the Piedmont match the Tidewater's list of famous citizens, but those who came from the region have no superiors. Thomas Jefferson was born at Shadwell, near Charlottesville, and left an imprint on that city that has not been equaled in more than two hundred years. His imprint on the United States is no less significant. Indeed, Jefferson is one of the American patriots best known abroad. George Rogers Clark, who saved the Northwest Territory for the United States, and the Lewis and Clark team who explored the vast territory between the eastern settlements and the Pacific Ocean, all were born in Charlottesville. The great black leader, Booker T. Washington, was born in a slave cabin in Franklin County.

*Mr. Jefferson's University*

The Charlottesville area sometimes is referred to as "Mr. Jefferson's country," and the university that he founded is often identified as "Mr. Jefferson's university." Charlottesville was settled about 1737, but remained mostly a stop on a popular frontier trail until Jefferson opened his university there in 1819. This was the making of the community; the university is still the largest industry in Charlottesville, and one of the principal tourist sights. Mention "the" university and any Virginian will know what is meant. Mr. Jefferson's university, preserved as part of the large institution that has grown up around it, is small. It includes a rotunda building for classrooms, two rows of dormitories, and pavilions for classrooms and professors around a "rectangle." It is still con-

**Northern Mockingbird**
A natural mimic, the mockingbird with his tail flipping jauntily can be spotted in both the towns and the countryside.

This classical rotunda **left** is the central building in the university designed by Thomas Jefferson in Charlottesville. Now part of the University of Virginia the original buildings are still in use—and the right to live in the first residences is a cherished student tradition.

Monticello, the home of Thomas Jefferson **right**, reflects the wide range of his interests. The classical appearance is combined with interior innovations that range from a dumbwaiter to an unusual clock in the entrance hall. Jefferson's experiments in agriculture also are acknowledged.

In the foothills of the Blue Ridge Mountains near the Rivanna River in western Virginia, Charlottesville **opposite** is beautifully located.

The **Jeffersonia diphylla** is one of the many plants to be seen in the gardens which brighten the east and west lawns at the Monticello home of President Jefferson. The gardens were restored to their original appearance in **126** 1939 and 1940.

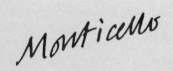

sidered an honor to live in one of the original rooms, despite the stares of tourists searching for the plaques that identify rooms used by Edgar Allan Poe and others. The rotunda no longer houses classrooms, but it is preserved as a museum.

The neoclassical style of the university is typical of Jefferson's architectural preference, which reached its zenith at Monticello, his home. This hilltop residence, made of red brick with a white dome, is one of the most impressive mansions in Virginia. It also has one of the finest views of the beautiful Piedmont countryside. Construction was begun in 1769 and Jefferson moved in while it was being finished because his father's home at Shadwell

burned in 1770. The imaginative mind of Jefferson never finished working on the house, and he incorporated many unusual features, from the seven-day clock in the entrance hall to the dumbwaiter in the dining room. The mansion, which attained its present form in 1809, reflects Jefferson's inquisitive nature and love of experimentation. Many of the objects displayed in the house were his. Jefferson's library ultimately was purchased as the foundation of the Library of Congress.

Jefferson's grave is located in the family cemetery, on the hillside approach to Monticello. In the epitaph he wrote for himself, he is remembered for three things: as author of the Declaration of Independence, as author of the Virginia Statute of Religious Freedom, and as father of the University of Virginia. The many offices he held, including the governorship of Virginia and the presidency of the United States, he was willing to leave to the judgment of future generations. Despite his many and varied accomplishments and his great contributions to the American nation, Jefferson never achieved the popularity of many of his contemporaries. He was so disliked by John Adams of Massachusetts, the story goes, that Adams on his deathbed lamented the fact that Jefferson still lived. Adams was wrong; Jefferson had died several hours before.

The hilltop site of Monticello looks toward the home of another president, James Monroe. Monroe moved there in 1789, with his new bride, in order to be near Jefferson. Ash Lawn is quite different from Monticello; it is not a mansion of the landed gentry, but a modest country home. The front of the house was added in this century, but the original part at the rear clearly reflects the simple, even primitive, life of the period.

This statue of President James Monroe **right** occupies a place of honor among the shrubbery at Ash Lawn. Monroe authored the doctrine that warned European powers not to colonize the Western Hemisphere.

# Charlottesville

A ride to rival that of Paul Revere, though not so famous, took place in the Piedmont region during the Revolutionary War. When Jefferson was governor of Virginia, British Colonel Sir Banastre Tarleton raided Charlottesville in the hopes of capturing Jefferson and members of the Virginia legislature, who had taken refuge there after the British attacked Richmond. Tarleston might have succeeded had not Jack Jouett been in a tavern at Cuckoo, thirty-nine miles west of Richmond. When he saw Tarleton's troops, he surmised their objective and rode posthaste to Charlottesville to warn Jefferson. Most of the members of the Virginia government escaped to Staunton.

Michie's Tavern, now a combination restaurant and museum, is situated on land sold by Patrick Henry to John Michie for a tavern

Ash Lawn **above** was just a simple farmhouse when James Monroe moved there to be near his friend, Thomas Jefferson. The original home is preserved intact, behind the front section added in this century.

The rolling fields of Loudoun County **left** nurture fine show horses and host numerous horse shows each year.

Castle Hill **above** has been in the Walker family for more than 200 years. Dr. Thomas Walker was the guardian of the young Thomas Jefferson.

Michie Tavern **below** still dispenses Colonial-style food, much in the way it offered sustenance to travelers along the Colonial trail to Charlottesville. Some of the structures are now museums.

on a well-traveled road. A colonial-style buffet is served in a two hundred-year-old slave house, while the other buildings house a good assortment of pre-Revolutionary War furniture and a number of household inventions. Castle Hill, privately owned, has been in the Walker family for two hundred years: Dr. Thomas Walker was guardian of the young Jefferson after his father died. An early eighteenth-century log cabin, relocated to a Route 20 site about a mile from Charlottesville, houses a George Rogers Clark museum. His more famous brother, William, and Meriwether Lewis are memorialized by a monument in Charlottesville.

The city's newest attraction is the Western Virginia Visitors' Center, a legacy of the Bicentennial celebration in 1976. Displays in the center explain the exploration of the western part of the state, including the nearby Shenandoah Valley and the Blue Ridge Mountains.

Patrick Henry's home at Scotchtown, near Ashland, is more a representation than a restoration. Henry was not much of a record keeper, so the way the Henrys used the house is not known. The personal relics are few and unimpressive; only two items have been

authenticated as belonging to the orator and statesman. This lack of personal identity does not detract from the house, which is an excellent example of the way the well-to-do lived in the Piedmont before and during the Revolution. The black walnut doors, superb paneling, and wide floor boards throughout the house are original from the Henry period. The basement includes one room, now decorated as a bedroom, about which something definite is known: it was used for a time as a family sickroom. Henry's last home and burial place is Red Hill, near Brookneal. The reconstructed

Confederate General Robert E. Lee surrendered to General Ulysses S, Grant at the little town of Appomattox Court House **above** on April 9, 1865. The town today is not that much different than it was more than a hundred years ago. The original courthouse burned in 1892. This structure is still a major attraction, although the actual surrender took place at the McLean House a little way off.

Patrick Henry lived at Scotchtown **left** when his oratory made him famous as a lawyer and patriot. The mansion is furnished in the manner of the period, but little is known about how it was decorated when Henry lived there.

house contains period furnishings, and his old law office also is located on the site. A boxwood maze and colonial garden are there as well.

## The Piedmont and the Civil War

Although the Piedmont had few strategic targets of great value, its location made it the scene of numerous bloody battles during the Civil War. The region is strewn with the litter of battle, now neatly packaged in national historic parks and individual shrines. The first major battle was fought at Manassas (also known as Bull Run), and Lee surrendered at Appomattox, after losing Richmond and Petersburg. In between are names that make peace-lovers shudder when they think of the carnage: Chancellorsville, Spotsylvania Courthouse, the Wilderness. The battlefields extend from north to south, but do not proceed chronologically; they resulted from a succession of federal invasions of Virginia. The battles literally drained the South of its manpower and wealth.

Along Bull Run, near Manassas, two of the most crucial battles of the war took place—a year apart. Lee recognized the strategic value of the area at the outbreak of the war, and ordered it fortified against Union invasion. Manassas lay across an important route to Richmond and kept open the approaches to Washington. First Manassas was the first major engagement of the Civil War, and it created an excitement that none of the later battles would. Men who had never experienced battle rushed eagerly into it. Civilians from the nation's capital took picnic lunches to the area in the summer of 1861 to watch the fighting. The battle identified one of the South's ablest generals and gave him the nickname "Stonewall." It was the last time crowds would gather to watch the spectacle of war. At Second Manassas, there were no spectators, nor eager soldiers, only those with the grim determination of men accustomed to war. Both battles ended in victory for the Confeder-

131

The Booker T. Washington National Memorial **right** honors the former slave who rose to become an important leader. He stressed the need for education for blacks and founded the Tuskegee Institute in Alabama.

The golden tobacco leaf **center** was literally worth its weight in gold during the Colonial era. Danville is still a major tobacco center, and hosts the annual world tobacco auctioneering championships.

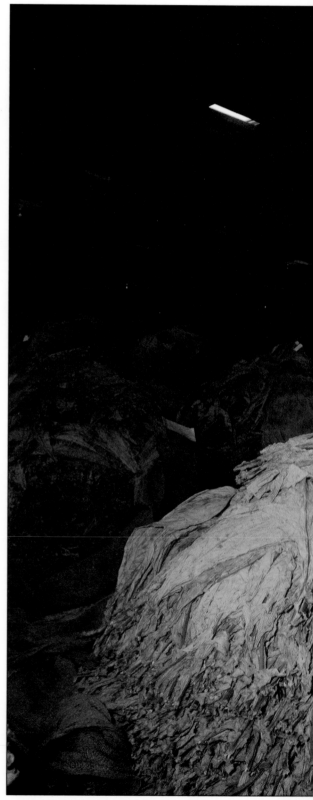

acy, and renewed calls for an invasion of the North. Lee's defeat was a disappointment at Antietam in Maryland, but his string of successes resumed at Fredericksburg and Chancellorsville. Lee invaded the North once more, but his defeat at Gettysburg and subsequent victories at the Wilderness and Spotsylvania produced manpower losses that could not be replaced, and opened the route to surrender at Appomattox.

There is a stillness still at Appomattox. Most visitors stand silently in the room where Lee and Grant met to work out terms of the surrender. The negotiators are still there, in the form of a large painting of the scene. Other museum buildings display stacked rifles and acknowledge the effort at reconciliation even then under way. Lee's magnificent message to his troops, some of whom wept openly at the news of surrender, is balanced by President Abraham Lincoln's unfulfilled promise of "malice toward none, with charity for all ..."

A few miles to the south of Appomattox, the Confederacy's viability ended when President Jefferson Davis and his Cabinet were captured. The building in Danville, sometimes called the last capital of the Confederacy, is now a museum and library.

Danville was already a major tobacco auction center when the Civil War broke out, and that role expanded in subsequent years until seventeen warehouses with 1.5 million square feet of floor space buzzed to the rhythmic calls of auctioneers walking slowly past huge bins of tobacco. The World Tobacco Auctioneering

The reconstruction of the tobacco farm where Booker T. Washington was born in 1856 **left** features the slave cabin he lived in and demonstrations of the chores of daily life in that period.

Championship, held annually in October, attracts auctioneers who chant as many as five hundred words a minute. The handsome houses on Main Street reflect the prosperity produced in the postbellum period by tobacco and textiles, the city's other principal industry. The popular ballad, "The Wreck of the Old 97," refers to an incident that occurred in Danville.

The Booker T. Washington National Memorial near Roanoke recalls the contributions to education made by the man who stressed vocational training for newly freed blacks and who founded Tuskegee Institute in Alabama. A visitors' center has exhibits and a slide show on his life, while costumed attendants work the small farm in the style of the mid-1800s. Nature trails also open up the 224-acre site.

Dams on the Roanoke River have created two primary lake resorts: Smith Mountain Lake and Kerr Lake. Philpott Lake on the Smith River near Martinsville is a smaller recreation area.

## The Northern Piedmont

The northern Piedmont, north of Interstate 64, is a sparsely settled but vibrant area. Though predominately agricultural, with numerous

This Clarke County farm
illustrates the continuing importance of
agriculture in Virginia. Tobacco
remains an important crop.

Gibson Hall Inn **above**, a bed-and-breakfast hotel in Upperville, was constructed about 1832.

Carter Hall in Milltown **right** is the privately owned headquarters of Project Hope. The home was completed in the eighteenth century.

The **hackberry**, which is found throughout the eastern United States, is a member of the elm family, but unlike the common varieties of elm bears an edible, cherry-like fruit.

horse farms and grain fields, the area has begun to attract light industry and "think tanks," which may expect the quiet and solitude of country living to improve the quality of their thinking. The horse farms extend from Orange County to Leesburg, in the northern part of the state, between Arlington and Winchester. Horse shows, like the Montpelier Steeplechase, show off the beautiful horses that can be seen grazing in the well-kept fields. Middleburg is sometimes described as the "capital" of Virginia's hunt regions. Loudoun County styles itself "Hunt country," with some justification. Both Oatlands and Morven Park are major horse centers, the latter the headquarters of the International Equestrian Institute and repository of the artifacts of the Master of Fox Hunt Association. One of the two large nuclear power installations in Virginia is located in Louisa County. A visitors' center at Mineral exposes the mysteries of turning atoms into energy.

## The Leesburg Area

Leesburg is one of the most picturesque communities in Virginia. A nine-block historic district concentrates twenty ancient structures, including a log cabin dating from about 1767 and the Loudoun County Museum. In the same area is an old stone house dating from 1759 that shows how indigenous materials were used in early construction.

Courthouse Square, scene of such landmark events as the signing of the Loudoun Resolves to protest the British Stamp Act, is one of Leeburg's most attractive features. It tells the city's history in a nutshell: The administration building, originally Leesburg Academy; an unusual iron gate; the statue of a Confederate soldier to indicate sympathies during the war; and the 1894 courthouse in colonial style to demonstrate the continuing impact of history on the community.

A walk around Leesburg is a fascinating lesson in diversity. Laurel Brigade Inn, still in use as a restaurant and hotel, dates from the 1760s. Among other structures are a store

Oatlands, a late Georgian house built in 1803, **left** carries on early traditions with an annual hunt and "Christmas at Oatlands," a display of Christmas ornaments made in the manner of the early nineteenth century.

**Overleaf** Morven Park is a beautiful mansion, but a johnny-come-lately. Its best feature is an extensive collection of antiques assembled by a Virginia governor, Westmoreland Davis, (1858–1942). The grounds include a fascinating carriage museum.

Piedmont farms, such as this
one at Purcellville **above**, have a special
ambience and a diversity of
interests. This one is one the fringes of "horse
country" as well **above right**.

operated by a sea captain during the Revolutionary War, two almost identical buildings from the same period, the 1790 bullet-scarred Fendall House, and the first property owned by Methodists in the United States. Many old structures are preserved by converting them to offices and stores, including a 1778 house that now serves as a real estate office. The oldest ecclesiastical building in the city is the 1804 Leesburg Presbyterian Church.

A few miles from Leesburg is Oatlands, built in 1803 by a grandson of "King" Carter and now owned by the National Trust for Historic Preservation. The interior has some unusual features, including an octagonal bedroom, and is furnished in antiques, many of them once the property of the owner. Each year, Oatlands hosts the equestrian shows of the Loudoun Hunt and the Virginia Foxhouse Club. "Christmas at Oatlands" features decorations made in the early nineteenth-century style.

Morven Park, also near Leesburg, isn't the standard Virginia historic home. Although part of the house dates from the eighteenth century, the principal attractions are the beautiful additions constructed much later and the furnishings and decorations collected by Virginia Governor Westmoreland Davis after he purchased the home in 1903. The dining room and French drawing room reflect the elegance of Davis's life-style. A half-portrait of Governor Davis, as Master of the Hunt in Loudoun County, presides over a collection of antiques that include six sixteenth-century tapestries re-creating scenes from the Punic Wars, a two-hundred-year-old Dutch clock, hand-carved Spanish writing desks that are about four hundred years old, and a mantel from the White House, purchased when President Theodore Roosevelt had the home of the president redecorated. The eclectic Davis collection presaged the modern habit of buying antiques for their own sake, without specializing in a special period or kind of article.

Morven Park's museum of carriages depicts the evolution of vehicular transportation. Among the 125 vehicles on display are horse-drawn carriages of various styles from several countries, fire engines, hearses, and even a 1965 Lincoln.

Sully Plantation, nearby, built in 1794, stands just as it was constructed, and is not a restoration.

Courthouse Square **below** structures represent critical periods in the history of Leesburg: the Revolution, Civil War, and modern. Leesburg protected precious documents, including the Constitution and Declaration of Independence, when Washington was burned during the War of 1812.

141

# WESTERN VIRGINIA

estern Virginia is the most distinctive geological feature in the state. Two rows of mountains, part of the great Appalachian chain, extend in a northeasterly to southwesterly direction, divided by a wide valley. The area has incredible beauty. The Indians worshipped the Shenandoah Valley as "the daughter of the stars." The Blue Ridge Mountains have a distinctive haze that inspired their unusual name, and there are spectacular physical features—Natural Bridge, Natural Chimneys, Goshen Pass, and many caverns. These sights have caused Virginians to wax poetical since Governor Alexander Spotswood uncorked champagne on the crest of the Blue Ridge in 1716 and founded the Knights of the Golden Horseshoe in honor of those who were with him. Strong men have been attracted to the region and, as long as men have been in the region.

Western Virginia was settled earlier than might have been anticipated. The seeds of settlement blew west as soon as the Jamestown colony matured. Inquisitive minds would not stop at the fall line of the James or Rappahan-nock, but continued to wonder what lay beyond the forest that stretched as far as they could see. When men reached the west, they explored the mountains and settled in the valley. The rich soil of the valley was a godsend to those who could not breach the mountains, but the ridges did not remain a barrier long. The discovery of the Cumberland Gap opened up the vast territory of Kentucky and beyond. The mountains were well enough settled by the end of the seventeenth century to begin creating their own legends. One of them concerns a frontier woman who reacted in a strange way to having her husband scalped by Indians. "Mad Ann" Baily, as she became known, turned to scalping Indians. In time, she turned her frontier savvy to better use by saving a settlement at what is now Charleston, West Virginia.

Tidewater men reched the valley first, traveling along the Germanna and Occeonee-chee trails, but they soon were joined by a different kind of settler who followed the convenient corridor of the Shenandoah Valley south from Pennsylvania. These people were

Autumn is a particularly beautiful time along the Blue Ridge Parkway **right**. Stunning vistas of the changing colors are around almost every bend.

**Opposite** Behind this Victorian door is Lee Chapel at Washington and Lee University. Inside is a recumbent statue of Lee over the Lee family crypt by Edward V. Valentine.

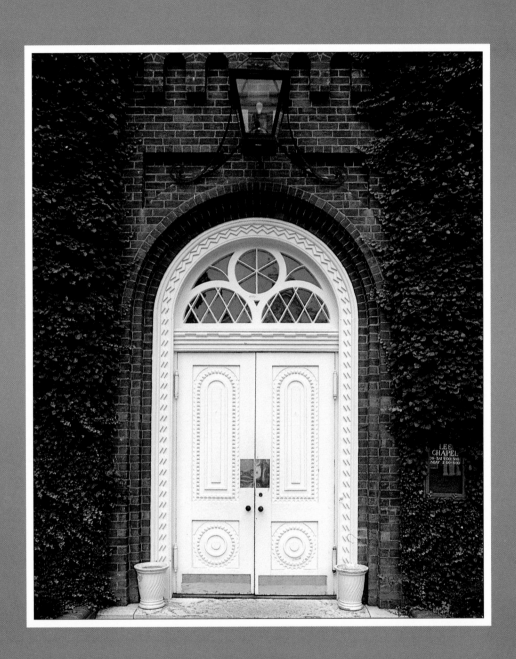

## E A R L Y  L O G
## C O N S T R U C T I O N

This simple log construction shown in detail above
was a very efficient solution to the problem of building with a few
simple tools and using locally available materials.
It provided shelter for frontier families and protection from Indian
raids. Many examples of early mountain homes still
exist using these techniques along the Blue Ridge Parkway.

The advance of communications and transportation rendered obsolete some of the services so essential to earlier periods, such as this abandoned grist mill **opposite**.

Scotch-Irish Presbyterians and German Lutherans, who differed in thoughts and desires from the Tidewater Anglicans. The trail they followed was an old Indian trail, but in time it became so foot-worn that it was named the Valley Pike. The families who populated the valley were equal to the hard life that nature and the Indians imposed on them. They read their Bibles and kept a gun near the plow; they started schools wherever they went; they planted roots along with their crops, as their rock houses showed; and they valued the freedom they could not have attained in the Old World. Few of them owned slaves. The Tidewater taste for conformity was not theirs. They asked few questions of their neighbors, and did not expect their neighbors to pry. They cooperated better than people in the cities did, but they did not congregate so easily as did those on the coast.

By the time of the Civil War, the Shenandoah was an indispensable breadbasket for the Confederacy. Vulnerable as it was to invasion from Washington, it was ably defended by relatively small forces. Thomas J. "Stonewall" Jackson, a professor at Virginia Military Institute in Lexington at the outbreak of fighting, proved his tactical genius by outmaneuvering his opponents in the valley. Jackson seemed to be everywhere, as he used his knowledge of wind gaps and his ability to inspire men to arduous marches to inflict defeats that diminished federal interest in the valley. Only late in the war were Union forces successful in con-

The discovery of Cumberland Gap **previous page** and **center**, whose wilderness is preserved in a national park, opened the western United States to settlement. Historical displays recreate some of the exciting past of the natural attraction. The breach in the Alleghany Mountains became a conduit for settlers in 1750; in 1755 Daniel Boone created the Wilderness road through the gap.

trolling this strategic area.

Western Virginia can be divided into two sections: the mountains and valley and the Great Southwest. The scenery and utility of both have attracted a new breed of migrants—tourists—who go especially for the outdoors experience, but seldom miss the historic relics. Skyline Drive and Blue Ridge Parkway give drivers easy acess to a better view than the one Governor Spotswood got after weeks of traveling. The Appalachian Trail offers a much slower version of the same experience, while other visitors relax in the sylvan setting of George Washington National Forest or Shenandoah National Park. The invention of snow-making machinery made possible ski resorts stretching from Bryce Mountain at Basye in the north to Fancy Gap in the south. The skiers and sightseers are just following the footsteps oif their ancestors, who visited the area for the healing waters of the spas. The Homestead at Hot Springs is the only premier spa in Virginia to survive as a commercial venture, but Massanetta Springs and "Old Sweet" continue to serve as church conference centers and camp grounds.

## The Shenandoah Valley

Shenandoah is an almost magical name in Virginia. Although actually a series of valleys, it has always been regarded as a single entity by those who went there to found neat, rolling farms raising grain, cattle, and poultry. To Virginians, it is "the" valley or the Valley of Virginia. It sometimes is called the Great Valley, or "Stonewall's Valley" in recognition of his extraordinary exploits there. But it is first and foremost the "daughter of the stars," the description chosen by the Indians who were the first to see the fullness of the night skies and the beauty of the landscape. Gazing at the stars at night, while the owls and crickets harmonize, or gazing at the mist on mountain clearings in the morning produces a real sense of communing with nature.

More than 400 miles of
hiking trails and the scenic
Skyline Drive **left** wind
through Shenandoah
National Park. The
unspoiled woodlands are
full of beautiful hollows,
ridges, streams and ponds.

The question most often asked by visitors
to the region is, how did nature contrive such
marvelous things? This is especially true at
Natural Bridge, carved over millions of years
by tiny Cedar Creek. A pathway under the 150-
foot-high arch reveals both the grandeur of
the natural phenomenon and the initials that
George Washington carved on the wall when
he surveyed it about 1750. Thomas Jefferson
once owned it, having purchased the 157
acres around it for twenty shillings of "good
and lawful money" in 1774. A sound-and-light
program there explores the seven days of
biblical creation. The active formations of the
caverns on the site have been on display since
1978. The path continues beyond the bridge,
and leads to a saltpeter cave used during the
War of 1812, a brief appearance by the Lost
River whose origins still are unknown, and to
tiny but beautiful Lace Falls.

Natural Chimneys at Mount Solon, twenty
miles north of Staunton, are another natural
phenomenon. Seven limestone pinnacles,
created half a billion years ago when the valley

Shenandoah National Park
is a vast scenic and conservation area in the
western mountains of Virginia.
More than a hundred types of trees grow on
the slopes of the mountains.

The Homestead, one of
the finest year-round resorts in the eastern
United States, caters to
skiers in winter. A number of ski resorts have
developed since World
War II in the mountains of western Virginia.

Grapes **above** and **opposite above** have been a food crop in Virginia since the earliest days; Jefferson had a vineyard and made his own wine. In the last decade vineyards have become the basis of a new wine industry. A dozen wineries now produce table wines.

Neat, productive farms **below** made the Shenandoah Valley **opposite below** the breadbasket of Virginia for most of the state's history. The economy of the state has diversified in modern times, but farming is still central to the valley's economy.

area began to sink, rise to heights of seventy to one hundred feet. The phenomenon has been known at least since 1834, when it was described in Southern Literary Messenger as "The Cyclopean Towers of Augusta County."

The major caves in the Shenandoah Valley vary in size and beauty. Five are open commercially, led by Luray caverns, which have made such formations as flowstones and stalagmites and names like "fried egg" and "bacon strips" household words. The world's only "stalagpipe" organ is located in this cavern, which makes it a favorite place for weddings. Shenandoah Caverns have numerous pools that reflect the unusual formations, and large rooms where the formations have enticing names such as Grotto of the Gods, Cathedral, and Diamond Cascade. A two-hundred-ton balanced rock, located in Giant's Hall, rests on three small points. The Dixie, Grand, and Skyline caverns possess their own charm.

The Shenandoah Valley has no large cities along its two-hundred-mile length. The modest ones that exist do not dominate the region, but harmonize with it. Winchester, Front Royal, Harrisonburg, Staunton, Waynesboro,

Lexington, and Roanoke all lie along Interstate 81, which follows the traditional trail through the valley. Covington and Blacksburg, the latter the home of Virginia Polytechnic Institute and State University, are farther west, off the beaten track.

Winchester started as a frontier gamin, but now has a passion for its roots. The city may possess the largest collection of log buildings in the nation. The most famous one was used by George Washington as an office while surveying the frontier for Lord Fairfax and during the French and Indian War, when Winchester was a logistics base. The cannon in the yard are period pieces, one of which was used to defend Fort Loudoun in 1758.

Lord Fairfax, who owned five million acres under a royal grant, has much less now. He rests in a handsome sarcophagus in the small yard of Christ Episcopal Church, a colonial parish whose present·building dates back to 1828. Winchester's most historic church is Old Stone Presbyterian, which has a plain, white interior regarded as a fine example of the colonial period style. The annual Christmas Eve service is a community tradition.

**Northern Cardinal** This bright red-crested bird is America's most spectacular finch. It can be seen in gardens and woodland edges.

The phenomenon known as Natural Bridge **left** is one of the natural wonders of the world. The bridge, which today actually supports a highway, was surveyed by George Washington and once owned by Thomas Jefferson.

Seven limestone columns **right** at Mount Solon, rising 70 to 100 feet, create an interesting spectacle known as Natural Chimneys.

Winchester has mansions to prove that its citizens did not long remain in log houses. Abram's Delight, built in 1754, is noted for its stone exterior and early American furnishings. The Jackson Museum, also an early home, is remembered as the headquarters of "Stonewall" during the confusing fighting at Winchester, which was taken and retaken seventy times during the Civil War—thirteen times in a single day. The headquarters of the Union commander, General Philip Sheridan, is now an Elks home. The large apple on the lawn identifies the region's most famous farm product, as well as the annual Apple Blossom Festival, which attracts national attention.

Belle Grove, near Middletown, is a post-Revolutionary War home of distinction. The beauty of the grounds and the 1794 mansion gives little indication of the carnage that occurred there during the Civil War. Six thousand men lost their lives in the Battle of Cedar

Creek. Belle Grove, owned by the National Trust for Historic Preservation, sponsors a Wheat Festival with mountain music and demonstrations of quilt-making, blacksmithing, and other crafts. An old-fashioned Christmas observance is held each year. Wayside Inn, a colonial rest stop at Middletown, continues to serve meals in a colonial setting and manner.

Front Royal, now best known as the gateway to Skyline Caverns, was a frontier landmark. Its name is of dubious pedigree, however. One feasible story is that British soldiers, billeted there during the French and Indian War, were ordered to "front the royal oak" during drill. Front Royal remembers its other periods better, at an archaeological park and Confederate museum.

Tiny New Market, within sight of drivers on Interstate 81 north of Harrisonburg, was visited by history on May 15, 1864, when Union and Confederate troops clashed. The battle had a substantial impact on the course of the war, and has become a sentimental favorite because the boy soldiers from Virginia Military Institute fought there. Aroused from their beds, the teen-age boys marched all night in the rain from Lexington to reinforce a meager force of Confederates blocking yet another federal invasion of the Shenandoah. As the boys moved into line, with their new uniforms and bright banners, they were teased and jeered by the hard-bitten Confederate regulars; when the battle was over, the regulars cheered the courage and prowess of the cadets, who stormed the hill alongside the regulars and captured the Union cannon.

The visitor's map at New Market has an intriguing identification on it—the Field of Lost Shoes. It identifies a rain-soaked place where mud literally sucked the shoes off the soldiers as they attacked. The battlefield is now a memorial, with a handsome Hall of Valor brightened by a colorful stained-glass mural by Israeli artist Ami Shamir. From its inception, the memorial has sought to depict the battle in a larger context, as the dedicatory plaque states: "This memorial is dedicated to the valor on the part of all young Americans in defense of their country, as exemplified by the cadets of Virginia Military Institute in the Battle of New Market, May 15, 1864." The battlefield is deceptively quiet; except for the Hall of Valor and the cannon emplaced on the hilltop, it might be any of the neat farms in that part of

The **American sycamore**, a variety of plane tree sometimes called the buttonwood because its fruit is packed into dense, hard balls, is the tallest broadleaf tree native to the United States. Found throughout the eastern part of the country, its hardwood is greatly valued by carpenters and furniture-makers.

**Overleaf** This Staunton farm is typical of the well-kept places in the Shenandoah Valley.

155

The Apple Blossom Festival at Winchester **right** attracts celebrities and national attention. It identifies the region's principal crop.

the valley. It has that look for a reason: the memorial also preserves Bushong's Farm, on which the battle was fought. The farmhouse and nine dependencies depict Shenandoah life in the mid-nineteenth century, especially the near self-sufficiency the times required.

Staunton, one of the numerous places in early Virginia named after ladies by gallant explorers, is one of the oldest communities west of the Blue Ridge Mountains. The strategic crossroads began to develop as early as 1732, and by 1800 had a population of one thousand, a substantial number for the period. Because of its relative isolation from the fighting, Staunton served for a time as a refugee for the Virginia legislature during the Revolutionary War. The arrival of the railroad in 1854 provided new economic impetus, but Staunton escaped damage during the Civil War and, thus, has a superior collection of nineteenth-century buildings. These include Mary Baldwin College, which opened in 1842; Stuart Hall, which began a year later; and the First Presbyterian Church manse, where a future president

of the United States was born. President Woodrow Wilson went from the white, two-storey Greek revival house at Coalter and Frederick streets to achieve international fame as president and peacemaker. The 1846 house is now a museum, housing a collection of gifts and honors received by the twenty-eighth president as well as many of his personal belongings. Rome, Italy, subtly equated Wilson with Washington by declaring him "first in war, first in peace." Carlyle, England, made him an honorary citizen. Among other objects are the tattered Bible where his birth is recorded, examples of his handwriting, photographs of him as a student, professor, and president at Princeton University, and various items from his two terms in the White House. One of the most famous paintings of Wilson depicts neither his wartime leadership nor peacetime negotiating, but shows him signing the Federal Reserve Act of 1913. A carriage house beside the formal garden at the rear of the house holds the 1919 Pierce Arrow that Wilson used as president.

## The Lexington Area

Two of Virginia's prestige institutions of higher learning, Washington and Lee University and Virginia Military Institute stand shoulder to shoulder on a crest in the city of Lexington.

The Washington and Lee campus, whose Greek revival colonnade is a national historic landmark, is one of the most beautiful in the state. The name of the university honors two men critical to its existence. Started as Augusta Academy in 1749, the ruin of the original building is not far from the present campus. The school became Washington College after a gift of canal stock by George Washington saved the struggling institution. It is a source of pride to the university that the Washington gift still contributes to the education of every student. Lee became president at the end of the Civil War, after turning down an offer to become president of Columbia University in New York City. Lee felt obligated to help rebuild the South, and he is buried in the family vault in Lee Memorial Chapel. The famous recumbent statue by Edward Valentine is in the chapel sanctuary. One of the most famous portraits of Washington, the Pearle portrait of him in a British colonel's uniform during the French and Indian War, hangs in the chapel.

Graduates of VMI have taken part in every major American conflict since the Mexican War of 1845, and come from many states. "Stonewall" Jackson taught there, and the only home he ever owned is preserved as a memorial. Jackson is buried in the Lexington Cemetery. Matthew Fontaine Maury, the "Pathfinder of the Seas," was a physics and astronomy professor at VMI. A student from Pennsylvania, George Catlett Marshall, served as armed forces chief of staff during World War II and as secretary of state and secretary of defense during the Cold War period. The Marshall Museum and Library, facing one end of the parade ground, houses his papers and personal momentoes, including his 1953 Nobel Peace Prize. VMI remembers the cadets who fell at New Market each May. As the roll

Conducted tours of Luray
Caverns reveal a multiplicity of cave
formations, from relatively
young thin stalactites and stalagmites to
formations millions of years
old that look like eggs, bacon and other
familiar objects.

The "stalacpipe" organ
is the only one in the world. The Cathedral
cavern where it is located
is a popular setting for weddings.

Jefferson National Forest **right** covers more than half a million acres in the Allegheny and Blue Ridge mountains. Spectacular views at any season are found from any of the many vantage points along the Blue Ridge Parkway.

The oldest state-supported military college in the nation, Virginia Military Institute is a National Historic District. The Cadet Barracks **opposite** were built in the mid-nineteenth century in the Gothic Revival style.

The **Southern magnolia**, a small evergreen which thrives on warm weather, flowers most profusely where it is sheltered by a wall.

**Overleaf** The Colonnade at Washington and Lee University is a national landmark. Both George Washington and Robert E. Lee were benefactors of the university. Lee gave up the presidency of a large Northern university to help rebuild the South after it was devastated by the Civil War.

call of casualties is called, the platoon leader responds, "Died on the field of honor, sir."

West of Lexington lies Goshen Pass, one of the most beautiful places in the valley. State Route 39 follows the rippling Cowpasture River for several miles through sweet-smelling flowers and trees that filter the sun's rays. The comparison with the Biblical Land of Goshen, from which the name derives, is not misplaced.

The American agricultural revolution began in an unlikely place—a plain, hilly farm in the Shenandoah Valley. The reaper that mowed the wheat on the vast plains of the Midwest, the plains that today produce so much grain it is a major national export, was invented at Walnut Grove farm in Rockbridge County. The farm exists much as it did when Cyrus Hall McCormick invented the reaper, although the simple stone and log structures have been turned into a museum. In the blacksmith shop, near the old mill, is a replica of the first reaper, as well as models of later improvements. McCormick took his invention to Chicago, and founded a great industrial empire on it. In the process, he changed the American farm picture for all time; whereas 90 percent of the

population was engaged in farming at the time, only 5 percent live in farms today.

The city of Roanoke, the largest in the Shenandoah Valley with approximately one hundred thousand people, marks the southern boundary of the valley. The city was a small community of four hundred people known as Big Lick in 1880, but developed rapidly after the Norfolk and Western and Shenandoah railroads both selected it as a site for machine shops. Roanoke is the most industrialized city in the valley. A transportation museum recognizes the industry that made it grow, but the city has made a concerted effort to improve its image. It erected a hundred-foot-high star on Mill Mountain and styled itself "Star City." Downtown improvements include Center in the Square, which is a restored 1914 warehouse converted into a museum, arts center, and theater. The science museum has exhibits on the natural development of the state, energy, health, and nutrition, and a planetarium. The city market, which opened in 1874, is one of the oldest produce markets in continuous use in the nation. These efforts are an attempt to live up to the reputation started a century ago by the Hotel Roanoke.

This faculty residence is
one of the historic buildings on the
Washington and Lee University
campus. The university, the sixth oldest in
America, was founded in
1749.

# Southwest Virginia

Hollins College, seven miles north of Roanoke, occupies the site of a once-famous resort, Botetourt Springs. The old stone springhouse dates from 1820, and even President Andrew Jackson visited the springs. Roanoke College, actually in the adjacent city of Salem, was established in 1842.

Southwest Virginia is coalfield country, and it's tough reputation is well known even to many who have never been there. Part of the Great Southwest also is known as the "Fighting Ninth" congressional district, but the prefix did not always refer to the political differences that existed among themselves and with the rest of the state. However, the Southwest has a gentler side, too. The Barter Theater of Abingdon was created during the dark days of the Depression and earned a national reputation. The advanced educational institutions, such as Emory and Henry, Ferrum, Sullins, and Virginia Intermont, have reputations for quality. The names of a few places—Meadows of Dan, for example—result from the religious devotion of the people who settled the region. But there were superstitions, too, and these became enshrined in the literature of the region. John Fox, Jr.'s "Trail of the Lonesome Pine" influenced American thinking about the mountain folks for many generations. The Fox house at Big Stone Gap, built in 1888, is a Virginia historical landmark. The dramatization of the play is still running at the June Tolliver Playhouse, named for the heroine in the play. Fairy Stone Park satisfies the love of mystery that exists in mountain folks—and in all of us to a degree. In that area, cross-shaped stones have been found lying on the ground. Lover's Leap recalls the Virginia version of a popular theme, young lovers who chose death over separation.

The Great Southwest has the most rugged outdoors areas in the state. Vast sections are dedicated to wilderness, sometimes with discreet public activities. Jefferson National Park and Mount Rogers National Recreation Area are the most prominent. Hungry Mother and Grayson Highlands state parks have been

packaged for modern comfort. The area is laced by small streams, and dotted with fish hatcheries. Attractions include the scenic Blue Ridge Parkway; Natural Tunnel, which pierces Powell Mountain; Mountain Lake, and old resort area; unusual rock formations called The Narrows and The Palisades in Giles County; the Cumberland Gap National Historical Park; and Breaks Interstate park.

The Blue Ridge Parkway begins at Afton, in the Shenandoah Valley, an extension of the Skyline Drive. The roadway follows the crest of the ridges at altitudes from 649 to 6,000 feet and ends at the Great Smoky Mountains National Park in North Carolina. Waysides present magnificent vistas and reveal both the geologic and the human history of the area. One of the locks of the James River and Kanawha Canal is preserved at the James River Wayside. Peaks of Otter visitors' center has an explanation of Southern Highlands wildlife and Indian history. Mabry Mill, near Mea-

Jackson Memorial Hall **left** at Virginia Military Institute is decorated by the flags of the 26 states in the union at the time the college was founded in 1839. A painting depicts the attack of the boy soldiers from VMI at the Battle of New Market.

**Sassafras** The aromatic twigs, bark and roots of this genus are used to produce fragrant oil and tea. Native to the east, it grows up to 75ft.

167

More than 1,200 varieties of flowering plants, including rhododendrons **left** grow in the western mountains of Virginia. Overlooks and trails are designed to give visitors easy access to wilderness areas where rhododendron, dogwood, and mountain laurel bloom profusely.

The foothills of the Alleghany Mountains are rich, as this farm **right** near Roanoke demonstrates.

**Ruby-throated Hummingbird** The only eastern species of hummingbird, this tiny creature is particularly attracted by red flowers.

dows of Dan, is a restored waterpower grist mill where demonstrations of everyday mountain crafts, such as the making of apple butter, are given.

Breaks is an example of interstate cooperation, as well as a reminder that boundaries did not mean much in this mountainous region. The canyon is sometimes called the "Grand Canyon of the South" because it is the largest east of the Mississippi River. The park's best-known feature is the Towers, created by an 180-degree turn in the Russell Fork of the Big Sandy River. Outdoor displays show some of the ways pioneers used the area. A corn mill still shows the way corn influenced the eating and drinking habits of the early settlers—food by the bushel, drink by the gallon. A huge, cast-iron pot was used to boil down salt from nearby mines for national defense during the formative years of the nation.

Cumberland Gap National Historical Park protects the natural gap in the mountains by

**Overleaf** Mabry Mill on the Blue Ridge Parkway preserves a facet of mountain life that is now virtually extinct. Ed Mabry and his wife "Boss" operated this hand-built, water-powered mill from 1910 to 1938. The mill has been reconstructed and is functional again.

Mountain crafts from the early part of this century are demonstrated at Mabry Mill, as this spinner **right** shows. Displays cover other facets of the self-dependant life.

which settlers spread into the interior of the United States. Daniel Boone was among those who walked through the gap and into the folklore of the nation. He blazed the Wilderness Trail, the principal route used by eighteenth-century explorers and settlers. Trails provide intimate glimpses of wilderness areas; a four mile scenic road leads to the park's most famous feature, Pinnacle Outlook. The museum at the visitors' center demonstrates both the violent and the peaceful sides of the frontier: Civil War arms and farm tools.

This, then, is Virginia, a state of great beauty, of great accomplishment, and of great tragedy. A state of mind, really, as much as a political entity, for courtliness and courtesy survive in an era when such things have been pronounced irrelevant. They are relevant in Virginia because they give Virginians a sense of identity with the past and an anchor for the future. Virginia is changing, in moderated ways, because the world is changing. But there is a sense of direction in Virginia's change. It is not the confusion of Matthew Arnold: "wandering between two worlds, one dead, the other powerless to be born" Rather it is the reflection of Lord Byron: "I am not now, That which I had been."

The Blue Ridge Parkway
follows the highest possible route through
470 miles of the southern
Appalachian Mountains. The highway was
designed for scenic enjoyment.
The road follows the natural contours of the
land, the speed limit is restricted,
and there are many scenic turnouts and
viewpoints.

# INDEX